BUSH CRAFT 101

BUSH CRAFT 101

A Field Guide to — the Art of — WILDERNESS SURVIVAL

Dave Canterbury

ADAMS MEDIA
New York   London   Toronto   Sydney   New Delhi

Adams Media
An Imprint of Simon & Schuster, Inc.
100 Technology Center Drive
Stoughton, MA 02072

For information about special discounts for bulk purchases, please contact Simon & Schuster Special Sales at 1-866-506-1949 or business@simonandschuster.com.

The Simon & Schuster Speakers Bureau can bring authors to your live event. For more information or to book an event contact the Simon & Schuster Speakers Bureau at 1-866-248-3049 or visit our website at www.simonspeakers.com.

Interior illustrations by Eric Andrews

Manufactured in the United States of America

35 2023

Library of Congress Cataloging-in-Publication Data
Canterbury, Dave.
  Bushcraft 101 / Dave Canterbury.
    pages cm
  Includes index.
  ISBN-13: 978-1-4405-7977-6 (pb)
  ISBN-10: 1-4405-7977-6 (pb)
  ISBN-13: 978-1-4405-7978-3 (ebook)
  ISBN-10: 1-4405-7978-4 (ebook)
1. Wilderness survival--Handbooks, manuals, etc. 2. Outdoor life--Handbooks, manuals, etc. 3. Outdoor recreation--Handbooks, manuals, etc. 4. Camping--Handbooks, manuals, etc. 5. Camping--Equipment and supplies--Handbooks, manuals, etc. I. Title.
  GV200.5.C37 2014
  613.6'9--dc23
   2014012976

ISBN 978-1-4405-7977-6
ISBN 978-1-4405-7978-3 (ebook)

DEDICATION

I would like to dedicate this work to all the frontiersmen and woodsmen who came before me who have passed on their knowledge through their writings and journals. Without these individuals we would not have so much information from which to glean our current knowledge, and without their dedication books like this one would be impossible.

CONTENTS

CHAPTER 3: ROPE, CORDAGE, WEBBINGS, AND KNOTS   69

CHAPTER 4: CONTAINERS AND COOKING TOOLS   85

CHAPTER 8: NAVIGATING TERRAIN 151

CHAPTER 9: TREES: THE FOUR-SEASON RESOURCE 169

CHAPTER 10: TRAPPING AND PROCESSING GAME 177

— Introduction —

"Preconceived notions, especially when one is fairly brought up in their influence, are most difficult to shake off."

STEWART EDWARD WHITE, *CAMP AND TRAIL*, 1907

"Bushcraft" is a term for wilderness skills and is the practice of surviving and thriving in the natural world. To effectively practice bushcraft, you must master a unique skill set that includes firecraft, navigation, trapping, creating shelter, tracking, and the use of tools, both modern and primitive. Wise hikers carry few essentials and tools with them on their journeys; instead of extra equipment, they carry the knowledge and skills needed to create necessary items straight from the landscape. To thrive in the woods without the modern comforts available today takes determination. Like any hobby, it requires dedication and knowledge that may in certain circumstances save your life. Many bushcrafting skills are essential to surviving in the wild in an emergency.

Turning to the not-so-distant past, you'll find that some of the most influential men in history took life in the wilderness as a serious endeavor as well as a euphoric pastime. They reconnected with nature, conserved resources, and worked to preserve the natural world. Theodore Roosevelt is perhaps the most famous president associated with exploration, preservation, and life in the wild. Working with John Muir, founder of the Sierra Club, he improved the protection of the United States' natural wonders, preserving 230 million acres of wildlife habitat across the nation. Within thirty years of the turn of the twentieth century, folks in the United States were rediscovering what it was like to spend time in nature and finding a release from the day-to-day life. Writers and authors such as Horace Kephart and E.H. Kreps captured this new craze by using the terms "woodcraft" and "camping." They followed in the footsteps of their predecessors such as George Washington Sears "Nessmuk," who was an innovator in tramping and traveling in the woods for recreation—not survival. More recently, Les Hiddins, the Australian "Bush Tucker Man," Mors Kochanski, the Canadian bushcraft and survival instructor, and Ray Mears, the famous English woodsman and instructor, have all brought the practice of bushcraft to contemporary audiences.

Why would anyone, in this era of modern conveniences and incredible technology, leave a comfortable life behind in pursuit of a simpler, but potentially hazardous, tramp in the woods? The reasons are many, and the benefits are numerous. Practicing bushcraft is a great way for you to enjoy the outdoors. If you feel you're trapped in an urban environment, a good tramp is a way to return to the wild, turn off your electronic devices, and escape society's constant pressures. In addition, the abilities you hone in the bush can become lifesaving skills when it comes to disaster preparedness and survival situations.

Nessmuk said it best when he explained, "We do not go to the green woods and crystal waters to rough it, we go to smooth it." That is a powerful statement, especially in this day of modern convenience. Many believe that to "smooth it," or to be comfortable, means that we need lots of gear and gadgets. In reality, you need very little equipment to succeed in the wild. Instead, you need knowledge of the natural world. This book gives you that knowledge in a short span of words, but it must be complemented by your own experience and time in the bush to gain your own "Doctorate in Woodsy Knowledge" (a term coined by Mark Baker).

This volume is the perfect companion for outdoor enthusiasts as well as those new to practicing bushcraft. It was written from personal experience, research, and many days and nights afield within several different environments and ecosystems. Guided by my experience, you'll discover all you'll need for expeditions, from preparing your pack to setting up camp to choosing tools and supplies. This handbook also includes clear instructions on navigating, fire-making, trapping, fishing, foraging, and more. You'll even learn the best ways to conserve resources, both natural and man-made. The tried-and-true instructions, tips, and tricks found here will give you the important bushcrafting skills you need to transition from indoor living to surviving—and thriving—in the natural world.

It is my belief that by understanding natural resources and learning about the items that make the difference between comfort and misery, you can attain an almost euphoric experience when spending time on the trail or in the bush. With this book as your guide, soon you'll be enjoying the wilderness as well—without the need to smooth it. To that end, I present this writing to you, inspired by my heroes and mentors of the past as reclamation and a more contemporary version of bushcraft from my experience in the eastern United States.

—*Dave Canterbury*

PART 1

Gearing Up

Chapter 1

YOUR PACK

"The man, who goes afoot, prepared to camp anywhere and in any weather, is the most independent fellow on earth."

—HORACE KEPHART, 1904

When you practice bushcraft, you are a self-contained unit: You must carry all you need on your back and on your person, everything necessary to sustain you for the duration of your trip. (You must also include anything you may need in an emergency.)

THE FIVE Cs

You can organize the essentials based on the **Five Cs of Survivability.** Within these five base elements are all the tools and knowledge you need to be prepared for emergencies as well as to become independent of the trappings of the urban jungle. These items are the hardest to reproduce from natural material, take the largest amount of skill to reproduce, and control the conditions that most directly affect your body's core temperature. (They can also be used to process raw items to help control your body's core temperature.) These items, along with your ability to dress for the current conditions and knowledge of the natural world, make it easy to pack a light kit and enjoy your time "afoot."

The Five Cs are:

1. **Cutting tools** to manufacture needed items and process food
2. **Cover elements** to create a microclimate of protection from the elements
3. **Combustion devices** for creating the fires needed not only to preserve and cook food, but also to make medicines and provide needed warmth
4. **Containers** to carry water over distances or to protect collected food sources
5. **Cordages** for bindings and lashing

These items, along with knowledge of the landscape and a few items to secure your food, will be the core of what you pack and carry. You can then add a few things for first aid, navigation, and repair to make your life "smooth" while on the trail and in camp. Does that mean you need a plethora of items that will be miserable to carry or will be so cumbersome as to make you regret the trip within a few hundred yards? No; rather you must choose the right elements for your kit, and you must ensure that these items are of the best quality. In addition, you must make sure that they will perform several needed tasks well.

CORE TEMPERATURE CONTROL, COMFORT, AND CONVENIENCE

The Five Cs are largely intended to help you control your core temperature, comfort, and convenience. When packing or creating your kit, understanding these elements will help determine which items are truly important and which are only added weight.

Your first priority in any kit is to maintain your bodily functions and core temperature in any weather condition. For this reason, items such as combustion devices, clothing, and containers to process water will be of the utmost importance. If you look at comfort, these are the items that you will want to provide a comfortable night's sleep. Sleeping at least four solid hours per night is crucial to enjoying your time afoot. (You can gauge someone's experience level in the woods by how well he or she sleeps at night.) Convenience items are those that you don't have to pack but you would like to bring along to make things enjoyable or to make some tasks a bit easier. By focusing on core temperature control and comfort when planning your packing, you will make room for convenience items that make for memorable times in the wild.

PACKS: AN OVERVIEW

Now that you know the philosophy of packing, you need something in which to carry your gear. There are many different packing configurations and brands on the market today, and the choices in colors and style are almost endless. I have never been a fan of packs with lots of pockets and compartments; whenever you look for a certain item, finding it becomes an ordeal. Keep things simple; our mentors of the past believed the same. The most basic carry means a **bed/blanket roll, rucksack, pack frame,** or **pack basket.** Some of these can be combined for further comfort or versatility. In the following sections, we'll consider a few improvised strategies for packing, as well as some more common options available today.

CARRYING YOUR WOOL BLANKETS

If you plan to use a wool blanket and not a sleeping bag, you will need a queen-size 100 percent wool blanket and a twin-size

100 percent wool blanket combined for bedding; this will suffice in temperatures all the way to freezing. To create this carry option, lay a **tarp** on the ground, folded in thirds (8' × 8' is a good minimum size). Then fold the queen blanket in half with the twin folded in half on top of that. To this you will add other elements of the kit that you won't immediately need, as they will be confined to this roll until you set camp. Spare clothing and some dry tinder are good things to put inside this roll for dry safekeeping.

Once the roll is laid out on the ground, fold in half a piece of rope or webbing of 12' length and place it at the end of the roll. Roll the rope up into the rest of the bedroll; when it's in the roll, a loop will extend from one side, and the two tails of the rope will extend from the other side of the roll. Feed these tails through the loop and tie them off. You will then need to strap the roll together by using two lengths of cordage around the outside of the roll, and knot them off. In this configuration, you can wear the roll as a single strap, or the rope can be divided to form a backpack-style carry.

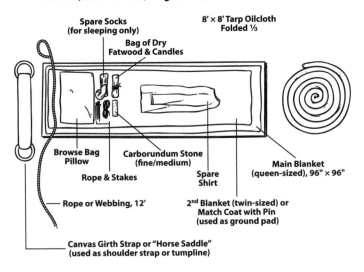

Blanket (folded in half, lengthwise)

Spare Socks
(for sleeping only)

8' × 8' Tarp Oilcloth
Folded ⅓

Bag of Dry
Fatwood & Candles

Browse Bag
Pillow

Carborundum Stone
(fine/medium)

Main Blanket
(queen-sized), 96" × 96"

Rope & Stakes

Spare
Shirt

Rope or Webbing, 12'

2ⁿᵈ Blanket (twin-sized) or
Match Coat with Pin
(used as ground pad)

Canvas Girth Strap or "Horse Saddle"
(used as shoulder strap or tumpline)

Assembling your bedroll

RUCKSACKS

A **rucksack** is a common name for a backpack, and there are hundreds on the market today. Again, lots of pockets and compartments in a pack can create problems; stick with designs that feature a large bucket-style compartment and a couple of outside pockets for easy access to important or often-used items. A pack large enough to fit a pack basket, or about 35–50 liters, is more than large enough for many days in the field. The most important thing to remember when selecting a rucksack is the overall durability of the pack and all its component parts, such as straps, zips, and buckles. Canvas packs are great, but a heavy material (with a denier of 500+) will work as well. For the beginner, military surplus is a good place to start. Military surplus materials have been tested to withstand much abuse, and if you inspect them, you'll usually find them to be in good order. They will serve you for many years at a very good price.

PACK BRANDS TO CONSIDER

When selecting a new pack for purchase, be sure the company has a good reputation and long-standing experience in producing packs. Remember: Your pack is your lifeline when you're off in the woods by yourself. A lifetime guarantee is money well spent. Duluth Pack Company has been in business since the late 1800s, and today holds to the same quality and guarantee as the company's creator. These packs are among the best if you choose a rucksack option. As far as surplus packs go, Swedish mountain rucksacks, U.S. ALICE (All-Purpose Lightweight Individual Carrying Equipment) packs, and USMC ILBE (Improved Load Bearing Equipment) packs are difficult to beat for time-tested durability.

Any pack system should include a waterproof bag large enough to fill the main compartment to ensure that contents are kept dry—no matter the conditions. After you've set up camp, you can remove the bag and use the emptied pack for gathering camp resources such as firewood. If you want to combine a rucksack with a bed/blanket roll option, the pack can be of smaller size; simply adding "D" rings from any saddle shop will allow the roll to be hung from the straps at waist level. Many of the packs and frames available include a waist belt that is padded to help distribute the load, and most can be removed if you find they are in the way or if you want a lighter load.

PACK FRAMES

Pack frames are my favorite system for carrying gear into the field. You can use them as a standalone item or combine them with other items. The versatility of external frames has been all but forgotten today. The most popular improvised frame today is the **Roycroft frame,** named after Tom Roycroft, an outdoorsman who taught the construction of this type frame to Mors Kochanski, the famous Canadian bushcraft and wilderness survival expert. This simple triangle can be constructed within minutes and can last many years if the lashings are correct and the wood selection is wise. To create this type of frame, first cut three components (easily made from a single hardwood sapling), and follow these lashing instructions:

1. Cut a lumbar slat or split piece of hardwood approximately 2" wider than the lumbar region of your back (or about the length of your armpit to your wrist).
2. Cut 2 pieces 1–1½ times the length of your arm from armpit to outstretched fingertips.
3. Shear lash (See Chapter 3) both longer components about 1" in from the ends of the lumbar slat, and then cross and diagonal lash them about 4" from the top to create a triangle.
4. Once the frame is complete, create 7 toggle points for tying gear to the frame. The strap for the frame is made from a 12' long

single piece of rope or webbing by making a lark's head knot passing through the top X of the frame. Then wrap the rope around the ears of the lumbar piece, tying around your waist to secure.

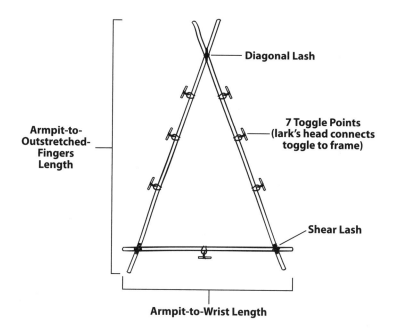

Roycroft frame

An advantage to this frame is that it does not have crossbars within the triangle frame, which would dig into your back. Other frame types with crossbars cause the pack's load to push through the frame and into the back, causing discomfort over time. To pack the Roycroft frame, you can use a similar method to making a bedroll. Again, use the tarp as the outermost component. Instead of rolling the gear up in the tarp, fold the tarp around the gear, ensuring that the last fold becomes a flap to shed water. Lash this to the frame using cordage in an X fashion, and tie it off with a jam knot or similar knot before adding straps and donning the pack.

Metal pack frames also come in many configurations and price points. A good cheap version (although a bit small for some things) is the surplus ALICE pack frame; you can find these with a complete shoulder strap and lumbar pad with waist strap for around $30. The only addition you'll need in order to use this as a standalone frame, similar to the Roycroft, is a few toggles for lashing points. In some cases you can also find a detachable radio shelf for the bottom of this frame, adding to its versatility. You can also purchase new pack frames made of metal tubes from companies such as Cabela's or Bull-Pac. These are made to carry game animals killed in the field. These frames are larger than the average pack and are mostly of good quality, although I would suggest checking these types of frames for the quality of their buckles, straps, and connections before purchasing. For a new frame, it is hard to beat the BULL-PAC, made by the company of the same name. This frame was designed with game carry in mind, but it has some qualities most regular frames don't offer: lashing points built into the design, with heavy and rugged hardware and straps, as well as a shelf to hold a bedroll secure. This pack should last a lifetime, and it is very comfortable even with the heaviest of loads (and lightweight when empty). Adapting these frames with other systems is a very easy process; one only needs to lash the gear to the frame itself and go (as with a Roycroft frame). I use the Bull-Pac design frame and incorporate many different systems depending on the excursion. A standard office trash basket makes a great trapping basket when attached to the frame, and with a bedroll nested on the shelf, it is a perfect hunting/trapping combination. Its size is dictated by the pack frame itself.

PACK BASKETS

Pack baskets have been used for many years, starting with the fur trappers of the Hudson's Bay Company in the late 1600s.

They generally come with pack straps attached and can be used by themselves as a pack or combined with other things. You can slip your pack basket into a large rucksack to make it more comfortable to carry. The advantage of the pack basket is its rigidity: It's easier to put things in and retrieve them later, and since the baskets are generally made from wood or woven from modern synthetics, they also drain well if anything you put in them is wet. Nonetheless, any gear placed into these baskets (other than trapping gear) should be placed in a waterproof bag, as with any pack.

In these packs you can carry metal traps, trap tools, and other gear without the chance of puncturing the canvas or other pack materials. When you combine a canvas pack outer shell, such as a Duluth Pack, an inner waterproof bag, and a pack basket, this becomes a very versatile system, providing three different carry options in one unit. You can set camp, remove the waterproof bag containing camp gear, remove the trap basket (a woven basket generally made from ash splits with added straps; it can be used as a pack) for use on a line while camped, and have the empty backpack to carry resources back to camp during short scouts for firewood, etc. All trapping components can be left in the pack basket, and any blood or mud from the trap line will be confined to the trap basket during use.

BUSHCRAFT TIP

A pack harness employs the removable strap system from a pack or frame to use with a load wrapped into a tarp or blanket. An example is a set of **ALICE pack straps** (widely available and very cheap when purchased through surplus stores). When used in conjunction with a wrapped load, such as a tarp and gear, the straps can be attached directly to the horizontal webbing or rope used to secure the package, thereby forming a simple but effective backpack.

TUMPLINES

Tumplines are straps attached to a heavier load (such as a pack or frame) that are worn across the forehead to assist in carrying the load. In the old days these were usually handwoven straps that were wider where they stretched over your forehead. Canoe enthusiasts of the twentieth century used tumplines many times to carry heavy backpacks from canoes when fording an area in which all gear and the canoe had to be transported from one navigable waterway to another (this is called "portaging"). An easy way to fashion a tumpline is to use the rope or webbing mentioned earlier and add a girth strap from a saddle between the lines. The girth strap is a padded strap for the girdle of a horse; this can be used as a padded shoulder strap tied in the middle of the tumpline from each end at the area to be used across the forehead. You can also repurpose this as a wider and more comfortable shoulder strap in conjunction with a bedroll. For the most part, in this day and age with the new designs of modern packs tumplines are unnecessary, but they can be useful when doing things in a more minimal fashion and trying to get the most from your gear. I can tell you that a tumpline comes in very handy when trapping, since you may be carrying a basket filled with about 100 pounds of the day's catch, in addition to your equipment. This alone makes its carry worthwhile if you're planning to trap.

HAVERSACKS

A **haversack** is a small bag carried on one side of the body. The haversack has been a standard carry item since the days of the frontier. These bags vary in size between 11" × 18" and 24" square; the exact size, however, is a matter of personal preference. Construction is usually of cloth or leather. Many haversacks are water-resistant, made from oilcloth or handmade waxed canvas. This device is used to carry items that are of immediate importance or items you collect along the journey. Never overstuff this bag to the point that you have no more room, especially for things you find along the trail; you may need room to store quick tinder sources or bird's nest material.

<table>
<tr><td rowspan="1">BUSHCRAFT TIP</td><td>Belt pouches, usually made of leather, are where the bushcrafter keeps his or her main fire kit and possibly a spare carving knife or jackknife. It is your wallet, so to speak, used to carry the most important items you may need, especially if you have left every-thing else behind at camp or if you lose your supplies. The size of this pouch is optional, but you don't want it so big as to become cumbersome while moving about.</td></tr>
</table>

PERSONAL CARRY KIT FOR THE TRAVELER AFOOT

Once you've selected your pack (or packs) you must decide what to put in it. The following is a general list of gear and supplies. This list is by no means exhaustive; however, it is a great reference tool to make sure you have the essential gear necessary on your journeys. Don't worry if you're not quite sure yet what some of these things are or what they're used for; I'll explain all of them as we go along.

POCKETS
❑ Jackknife
❑ Compass
❑ Lighter

BELT
❑ Sheath knife
❑ Kuksa (traditional wooden cup) on toggle

BELT POUCH

- ❑ Sun glass
- ❑ 4" × ½" ferrocerium rods wrapped on the end with 1" duct tape
- ❑ Spare lighter
- ❑ Carving jack
- ❑ 10' #36 tarred mariner's line

HAVERSACK

- ❑ Watch coat (oilcloth)
- ❑ Kerchief (linen)
- ❑ Cordage (partial roll of #36 tarred mariner's line)
- ❑ Work gloves (leather)
- ❑ Spare ferrocerium rod (6" × ½" end wrapped with 1" duct tape)

PACK

- ❑ 8' × 8' oilcloth tarp
- ❑ Large (55-gallon) plastic trash bag
- ❑ Twin wool blanket
- ❑ Queen wool blanket (or military Modular Sleep System [MSS] bag and bivvy)
- ❑ S.A. Wetterlings hunter's axe
- ❑ 1 roll #36 tarred mariner's line
- ❑ Folding saw or 20" bow saw
- ❑ Bush pot
- ❑ Skillet
- ❑ Waxed canvas bag with 3 beeswax candles and 6 sticks of fatwood
- ❑ Candle lantern
- ❑ Notebook and pencils
- ❑ 2–3 full lengths of hemp rope, ½" diameters
- ❑ 25' #550 parachute cord (ridgeline)
- ❑ Repair kit for knife and axe blades, straps and webbing, or canvas
- ❑ 10' #8 tarred mariner's line

❏ 2 sail needles, #9 and #13

❏ 1 Lansky's diamond rod

❏ 1 small whetstone

❏ 2 16P nails

SUMMER FISHING KIT (SMALL)

❏ 2 rigged lines, 1 fly line floating and 1 braided line with #6 hook

❏ Small vial of split shot

❏ Assorted hooks

❏ 3-prong metal frog/fish gig

WINTER TRAPPING KIT

❏ 3 #110 body grip traps

❏ 2 #220 body grip traps

❏ 1 #3 double long spring trap

❏ 12 assorted snares

❏ 25' baling wire

❏ Firearm and accoutrements (seasonal)

TIPS AND TRICKS FOR YOUR PACK

1. Used girth straps for horses make great tumplines and can be found cheap at local tack shops. These are made to last and have heavy metal rings that will support very heavy loads if needed.

2. If you are allergic to wool, alpaca is a great alternative material; however, it will generally not be as water-resistant as wool.

3. When experimenting with your kit, take a trip to the woods for a night, and when you return, reassess what you did not use. Unless circumstances dictate otherwise, leave it out the next time. If you find you need it, you can add again later.

4. Remember to always think outside the box about uses for the items you carry. In general, every item should have three uses, but the more you find, the fewer items you will add later.

5. Waterproof bags of 5–10 liters are always a good addition to both separate and waterproof essential elements of gear. They can also serve as containers for water collection and storage before and after boiling or collecting rainwater.

— Chapter 2 —
TOOLS

"In the early days of American life the Ax and Knife were the two indispensable tools ... With the knife they made spoons, brooms, rakes, and bowls; trimmed the skins of the animals they caught, and made the smaller things they needed in the cabin or around it."

—PHILIP D. FAGANS, 1933

Quality, well-maintained tools can mean the difference between an enjoyable, comfortable tramp and an unsuccessful—or even dangerous—venture into the bush. Remember from Chapter 1 that cutting tools are one of the Five Cs. This means they are essential items when practicing bushcraft. Because there are so many options when it comes to knives, saws, and axes, this chapter will give you the knowledge to select the best tools for your needs and particular destinations.

Caring for your tools is also a crucial skill set to acquire. It is not enough to carry these tools in your kit; proper maintenance will guarantee the longevity and durability of your tools over time. Equally important are your skills in properly handling, using, and safely dealing with your knives, saws, and axes. From sharpening edges to processing firewood to felling trees, this chapter details the essential skills you'll need to become an expert woodsman while protecting yourself—and those around you.

KNIVES

A belt knife is the most important tool any woodsman can own. This being the case, you must keep this tool directly attached to your person to keep it from becoming lost. With this item, you can recreate all other items you need, should an emergency arise. Therefore the ultimate question is, What is the perfect knife? Speaking from experience, I'd say it is usually the one you have on you when the need arises. However, for purposes of this discussion, let's examine the qualities of a knife that will be most useful to you in the wild.

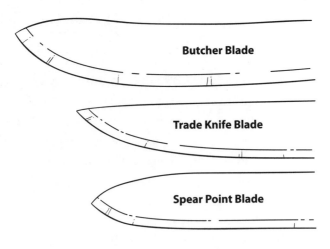

Butcher Blade

Trade Knife Blade

Spear Point Blade

Basic knife blade profiles

Begin by looking at the length of the knife blade. A blade that is too small will make it difficult to process firewood, if needed, especially if you are not carrying an axe or if one is not available. A blade that is too big will make finer carving tasks more difficult. The happy medium is about 4½–6" in blade length. Historically, most knives found along the American frontier were within this length and had the profile of a large kitchen or butcher's knife. These days blades made from high-carbon steels like 1095 and 01 tool steel are preferable, because of their ability to throw a shower of sparks (much like fire steel). This makes them excellent fire-starting tools. You can use high-carbon steel blades with a hard rock, like quartz or flint, to ignite charred cloth or material, especially if your preferred fire-making method fails or has been used up. The blade spine must have a nice sharp 90° edge; make sure it is not rolled or beveled. Again, this will allow you to use it as a striking device for the metal match or ferrocerium rod.

Many knives today are coated with something to keep blades from rusting. You should avoid coated knives; it is very difficult for knives with this coating to throw off a shower of sparks or ignite material in combination with a hard rock. It is better to just maintain your blade to prevent rust.

Any knife you carry as a belt knife should be of full tang design; this means the entire knife is one piece of steel with handles attached to the outside by a pin or screw. This is very important since the knife may take much abuse when processing firewood, especially while being struck on the spine while batoning wood (see following). Because your belt knife is such an integral part of your kit, you should reserve a considerable portion of your kit's budget for this tool.

The **knife grind,** or the shape of the cross section of the blade, is another consideration that boils down to personal taste. The main grind types are:

- Hollow Grind
- Convex Grind
- Flat Grind
- Scandinavian Grind

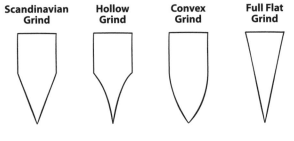

| Scandinavian Grind | Hollow Grind | Convex Grind | Full Flat Grind |

Basic knife grinds

Flat and **Scandinavian** grinds are easier to hone to sharpness quickly in the field. They split well but can be brittle, depending on the knife, if twisted side to side, especially in cold weather. They are absolutely the best for fine shaving and carving work. **Hollow**-grind blades will maintain a very sharp edge and excel at skinning tasks but are the most susceptible to damage because the blade is thin. **Convex** edges are the most resilient and best for splitting; however, they are more difficult to maintain in a field environment and not as good for finer tasks.

BUSHCRAFT TIP

JACKKNIVES (FOLDERS)

Many types of tools fit into the **jackknife** category, from **Swiss Army Knives,** to multi-tools, to the most expensive of single-blade folding knives. It is important to understand what this tool will accomplish for you, and to choose a knife that is as multifunctional as you need. Before purchasing any pocket-type tool or folding implement, think of it primarily as a knife.

Considering Multi-Tool Functionality

The main problem with most multi-tool knives on the market today is that although they're very useful as far as other tools go, their functionality as a knife is severely lacking. Harriet Simpson Arnow's book *Seedtime on the Cumberland*, published in 1960, tells of a gentleman carving a rifle stock for his broken flintlock with his whittling knife by the campfire. I cannot imagine attempting this task with today's multi-tool knife blades, as they are generally smaller and more flimsy than a traditional jackknife-style blade and much less utilitarian. Some Swiss Army–style folding knives have decent blades, however, and they offer other useful tools as well. The Boy Scouts used a camp-style knife for many years, and even the U.S. military adopted this configuration. This camp-style knife includes a nice blend of tools with a useful smaller blade for finer tasks.

JACKKNIFE SKINNING ABILITIES

Expert Horace Kephart states that if you intend to use this tool for skinning, your jackknife will require a keen blade that is also very durable. Many of our forefathers carried jackknives with multiple blades for such purposes. Today, there are several styles of jackknives made by companies such as Case and Imperial, including the Hunter, the Stockman, and the Trapper styles. For the purpose of skinning, I prefer the Hunter models, which employ two blades: one smaller blade for fish and fowl, and one larger blade for skinning mammals. These blades are approximately 3½–4" and are a good smaller tool when coupled with a 5–6" sheath knife. Any jackknife you carry should contain the tools that are important to your individual needs and be of the best quality.

KNIFE SAFETY/SAFE GRIPS

Once you've chosen your knife, it's essential that you learn to handle it safely. The last thing you want in the wilderness is to injure yourself (or anyone else) through carelessness.

THE TRIANGLE OF DEATH

The **triangle of death** is the space between your upper legs, including the groin and both femoral arteries. Avoid this area with an exposed blade at all costs. Never cut into this area or hold objects to be cut or carved in a manner that could cause the blade to enter it.

> **BUSHCRAFT TIP**
>
> If you are not alone in your excursion into the wild, any time you prepare to use your belt knife you will need to evaluate your **blood circle**. This is the area 360° around you and farther than arm's length, where someone could come into contact with a blade being pushed away from the material being cut.

IMPORTANT SAFETY TIPS

Safe handling practices with your knife in the field are of utmost importance. For this reason, place your belt knife immediately back into its sheath when you're not using it. Never place it on the ground or on another piece of gear. Always grip your knife as if making a fist; this will not only give you leverage and control but it will eliminate any chance of fingers contacting the cutting surface. If you must choke up on the blade of your knife for a finer carving task or for using the tip of the knife (as when making a notch or carving a net needle), you should wear leather gloves if available. Practice with your knife will make you more comfortable, but don't replace caution with complacency. A sharp knife is a double-edged sword: capable of the finest of carving tasks, but also capable of inflicting a deep wound and leaving permanent damage.

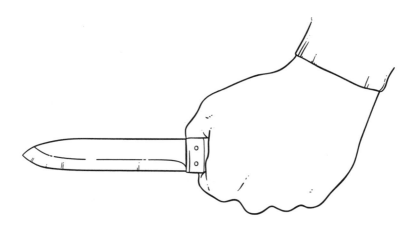

Safety knife grip

There are two good ways to make your belt knife work for you more efficiently and with more control, as opposed to a free cutting motion where the knife is pushed away from the work:

1. **The knee lever.** Lock your wrist holding the knife into your outside or opposite knee while in a kneeling position. Then draw the material toward the blade, removing material without movement of the knife itself. This method is especially good for taking off large amounts of wood, as well as for finer carving of points and things on tent stakes.

2. **The chest lever grip.** Point the knife outward while the arms holding both material and knife are levered like chicken wings from the chest, using the back muscles to control and remove material by moving the object to be cut and the knife blade simultaneously. This is a particularly effective method for removing heavier amounts of material while others are in close proximity.

BATONING

From processing firewood to making notches, you may find the
need to baton with your belt knife. **Batoning** is a method of cutting and splitting wood; you use a baton, or stick, to strike the
spine of your knife and push or drive it through a piece of wood.
This can be particularly effective when creating finer kindling
from larger material that may be wet or damp on the outside but
dry on the inside. To properly baton with your knife, you will need
a baton; usually this is a hardwood branch approximately as long
as the distance from your armpit to your palm. Softer woods will
damage easily, sending loose pieces of wood flying and causing
potential for injury to the eyes. If possible, place the material to be
batoned on a flat surface. This will give a steady base and will prevent your knife blade from coming in contact with dirt or rocks
by accident. Once the log is stood end-cut up on a solid surface or
anvil stump, place the blade of your knife in the position you wish
to cut or split the wood. Strike the spine of the knife with your
baton, and this will cause the wood to split at the desired mark.

BUSHCRAFT TIP

Woods with a lot of grain, such as oak, may tend to split
unevenly from a straight cut; you can counter this somewhat
by twisting the blade of your knife away from the runoff while
batoning. If you do not split the wood on the first strike, or the
knife goes below the plane of the top of the desired piece, you
may have to baton again, striking farther toward the tip of the
knife on the spine. This is another reason why you must have a
high-quality blade. Never attempt to baton a piece that is any
larger in diameter than the length of your knife, and try to stay
at least 1" in diameter smaller, if possible. If on occasion you run
into a knot or something that stops the travel of your blade,
insert a wooden wedge above the knife. Strike the wedge with
the baton; this will release the blade and often split the wood
completely.

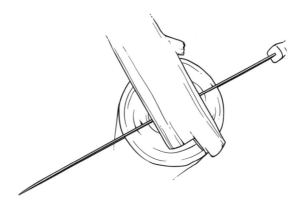

Batoning a branch

NOTCHES

The ability to carve certain **notches** in wood is an important skill; you'll use this ability for a multitude of camp needs. There are four notches that you will find most useful.

THE STAKE NOTCH

The **stake notch**, along with the stake's point, will serve you well for making not only tarp stakes but also trap components. To create this notch, select the material and length desired for the project, and decide the location of the notch. Place the material on a solid anvil, and baton a stop cut (that is, a cut that stops against another cut) one-third of the diameter of the wood at the desired top of the notch. Then, using your belt knife and a knee lever grip, step back about 1" from the stop cut, and remove material at a 45° angle toward the stop cut to finish the notch.

THE V NOTCH

The ability to create a **V notch** is a very useful skill when using toggles for any number of things—from tarp lines to pot hangers (a toggle is a small wooden stick hanging from a rope and used as a means to suspend things; see following). This notch helps lock a piece of cordage to the desired area of a toggle. It can also be used on a larger scale to keep material that is stacked from moving if the diameter of the notch is equal to the stacked material or if the piece of wood to be used in conjunction with this one is notched in the same fashion. This notch is similar to a "log cabin" notch (see following), but angled and not as precise in depth or shape. To create this type of notch, select the desired material and place it on a firm surface horizontally. Then, place your blade at a 45° angle and baton the knife blade to a depth of ⅓–½ the diameter of the wood, depending on the use to be made of the notch. Move to the opposite side of the notch, and repeat the process, creating a "V." For notches that will be under stress and not stacked, never cut these notches more than one-third the diameter of the material.

THE LOG CABIN NOTCH

The **log cabin notch** is used mainly for building; it can be used on a small scale to assemble a pack frame or on a large scale to build a cabin. To create this notch, baton the width of the desired notch with stop cuts deep enough to mate the desired piece. Once the stop cuts are made, remove the material in the middle with a knife or small wedge. Remember, when making notches that mate (just as with any building project), you can take away material but you can't add it if you make your notch too big—so be careful. Measure twice and cut once.

THE POT/BAIL NOTCH

The **pot/bail notch** is useful for making cooking tools. It can be used to support the bail (the wire handle) of a pot and inverted to make an adjustable hanger for moving pots closer to or farther from a flame or coal bed. This notch is a bit more complicated, but you can make it with these simple instructions.

Begin by making two stop cuts one-third of the way through the desired material in an X pattern horizontally. Then, use your knife and a knee lever grip to undercut and remove the bottom or top of the X, depending on the application, to leave a slightly undercut point. If this notch is made correctly, it will hook onto the bail of your pot when made close to the end of the stick or material. If the stick is inverted, changing the direction of the notch, and the notches are spaced apart by several inches, they can serve as a height adjustment by using a cross stick and drilling an indention in a wedge-flattened area at the end. This will create an area for the point to rest, thereby hanging or suspending your pot.

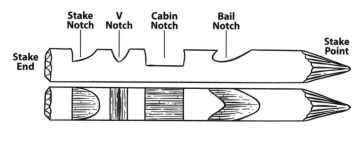

Basic notches

SHEAR CUTS

The object of a **shear cut** is to shave larger amounts of wood while maintaining control of the material and the knife. Making shear cuts requires an anvil of some kind to make sure the desired materials are steady and will not move side to side or slip. To create an anvil in a fallen tree, make a large log cabin notch in the fallen tree, and use the flat surface for your anvil. This way, you will not place the material being cut on a curved surface.

Shear cutting can be very useful when making feather sticks, very fine curled shavings of wood (see following); it is also great for cutting saplings with your belt knife if an axe or saw is unavailable. You can complete the cuts using one of two methods:

1. For small items, such as feather sticks, grip the knife with your fist, place your fist on a solid surface or anvil, and slowly draw the material toward you. By controlling the material's angle, you can create very fine shavings of the material.

2. If power is needed, as when you want to cut a sapling, use this method: Stand over the desired material, making sure it is anchored to an anvil (or in the case of a sapling, make sure it is securely in the ground). Using your upper body weight, push straight down into the material by moving your arm at the elbow only, with your body weight centered over the top.

CUTTING A SAPLING WITH A KNIFE

Cutting down saplings with a knife should be a last resort, something you should do because you do not have an axe or saw or because you cannot find deadwood to accommodate the needed task. To cut a sapling, you need to place stress on the tree by bending it over and using multiple shear cuts to beaver chew though it.

> **BUSHCRAFT TIP**
>
> A **beaver-chew technique** employs multiple cuts around the circumference of a stick to weaken it toward the center. It's similar to how a beaver cuts down a tree, only you're using your knife instead of your teeth.

As long as you're using a good, sharp knife, the process is pretty easy, but you must take care. Cut the tree as low to the ground as possible to avoid having the stump spring up and hit you. A larger stump can also be a trip hazard in the night. To top a sapling for use in shelter building or thatching (that is, trim the smaller branches toward the top), bend the top of the tree down and around, creating a "C," and stand on the top of the tree. While controlling the trunk under the arm, use the same shear cut and beaver-chew technique to top the tree.

BARK REMOVAL

Bark removal is necessary for most projects, but is especially important when processing inner bark materials for tinder materials. To remove bark, anchor the material on a good anvil and use the back of your knife in shearing fashion. To make finer shavings of inner barks, fatwood, and funguses, or to create fuzzy materials for tinder, you can use the same technique with adjusted pressure and angle.

> **BUSHCRAFT TIP**
>
> Your knife's edge is a resource, and all resources should be conserved—you never know when emergency could strike and prevent you from getting home when you planned. Another good reason to have that sharp 90° spine on your knife is for ease of bark removal and tinder processing using barks or fatwood.

FEATHER STICKS

Feather sticks can be used as a tinder source for your initial fire lay. They can help establish a fire faster. Create them using softer woods, which are more combustible because they're less dense. Feathered sticks increase the surface area with which heat comes in contact, making it more likely the fuel will ignite. Shear cuts on an anvil or a knee lever are both good techniques for making feather sticks. On larger branches of softer woods, you may need to stand upright when creating the feathers. All feathers should be created on the same plane as the wood. After creating a feather stick, if you can further reduce the shaving's size, making it about matchstick size, these will work the best.

Make up to twenty of these matchstick-size feather sticks, and use them at the base of the fire lay for a tinder bundle. Feather sticks of fatwood will make a great match for lighting the fire, reducing the time you need to use the open flame of a lighter. The general rule of thumb is that you should never need more than five seconds of flame from a lighter to obtain ignition. Feather sticks will help with this.

KNIFE CARE

It's of great importance that you keep your knife sharp and handle it with respect. It's among the most important tools any bush-crafter has.

PROTECTION

Protecting your knife means caring for it so that it does not rust from extended periods of exposure to damp. The best way to accomplish this is to dry the knife with your cotton bandanna or kerchief before replacing it in its sheath after use. Lubrication on the metal surface will help the blade repel water and also protect it from rust. Choice of lubricant depends a lot on your intent for the blade. I use olive oil to keep my knife lubricated. This is because when I'm processing foods, the knife is never contaminated with petroleum products such as machine oils. If you don't intend your knife to come into contact with food, machine oils will do the lubrication job as well.

SHEATHS

There are many different styles of **sheaths** on the market today. The two most common materials for sheaths are leather and Kydex. Leather is the traditional choice. Its biggest advantage is that it can hold lubrication within the leather itself over time, so that the knife is lubricated as you place it in the sheath. The biggest disadvantage of leather is that once saturated with water it holds moisture for a long time. To prevent this from happening or at least slow the process, soak your sheath in olive oil at home for about twenty-four hours, then allow it to drip dry before use. Or, you can wax the sheath with beeswax and heat the leather near a fire or other heat source, forcing the wax to impregnate the leather's pores.

The biggest advantage of Kydex—which is a moldable type of acrylonitrile butadiene styrene (ABS), a thermoplastic—is that it drains well if built correctly and is virtually indestructible. The downside to Kydex is that the closeness of the fit creates a tight, hard space that can trap debris. Any debris that gets into the sheath will likely scratch the blade when you move the knife in and out. Kydex holds your blade very well, keeping it secure from loss; when using a leather sheath, purchase one that has a flap over the knife handle that snaps in place and secures the knife at all times.

SHARPENING

You must regularly sharpen your knife to re-establish a worn edge. A dull knife is worse than useless; it's dangerous, since it's harder to control. The sharpness of your knife is a key indicator of your skill level as a bushman.

Whetstones

A **whetstone** is a sharpening stone, a tool used to remove metal from the blade of your knife to create a sharp cutting edge. Whetstones are the age-old method of sharpening or bringing the edge back to a knife. Any sharpening process involves a couple of steps.

First you must understand the actual degree of bevel that the cutting edge of your knife has; it will generally be at an angle of between 10–20°. The sharpening process is divided into five stages:

1. Coarse
2. Medium
3. Fine
4. Honing
5. Strop

A knife maker once told me that you should "sharpen your knife once and hone it forever." Although that's true, remember that each step of the sharpening process using coarse, medium, and fine abrasives removes metal from the blade with every stroke.

BUSHCRAFT TIP

Most whetstones were traditionally used with oil as a lubricant, but water is a much better substitute for trail and camp use. Just remember that when you buy a new stone, if you apply oil to it once, you can never go back to using water.

Stones come in different grits, from coarse to medium to fine, and are usually numbered by grit. (The larger the number, the finer the grit.) For example, an 800 grit stone is considered coarse and used for only heavy removal of material, such as large burrs. A 3,000 grit stone, on the other hand, is an ultra-fine grit for final finish work and honing of the knife. In general, I use about 1,000–1,200 grit stones for any routine sharpening, followed by a strop with a good leather belt. To sharpen your knife, you should first let the stone soak in water a bit, allowing all its pores to fill. Then, lay it on a flat surface or create a stand from wood that will keep the stone level. You can also use small nails to temporarily hold it in place on the flat surface you have created on a log or stump. Once the stone is in place, drag the blade of your knife at an angle determined by the grind (see following) across the stone, from the area closest to the handle toward the tip, maintaining the same angle throughout the stroke.

In sharpening a blade, carefully consider its current condition. If you use too coarse an abrasive, you are wasting a resource by removing more metal from the blade than needed, causing unnecessary wear. If you properly care for your blade, it should never take more than the last three steps—**fine sharpening, honing,** and **stropping**—to maintain a keen cutting edge. Using a whetstone will cause a burr (a thin piece of metal pushed to the opposite side during the sharpening process) to form on the opposite side of the blade; removing this will require even amounts of strokes on both sides of the blade as you progress. The rule of thumb here is that you will want two times the number of strokes for each successive step; if you use twenty strokes per side on a fine stone, then it will need forty per side on the honing stone, and eighty on the strop. Once you have obtained a good mirror finish, the blade should be good and sharp if the angle was held correctly.

Remember with stones to always use a water soak before use. Although oils have been a standard for many years in the field, oils will clog the pores of the stone and make cleaning the metal materials difficult. Water will alleviate this issue, and the stones can simply be rinsed in water. A light coat of light oil such as olive oil or animal fat will keep the blade protected after sharpening. The angle at which you hold the blade while sharpening will depend on grind angle of the blade itself.

Diamond Boards and Rods

Many folks today use a **diamond-coated card** or **diamond rod** for sharpening purposes, although most diamond-coated implements are about equal to a medium/fine stone. I have used them quite frequently in the field for quick sharpening. They are easy to pack, make the blade plenty sharp for your field needs, and don't require as much space as carrying multiple stones. You make a sacrifice here in the honing department, though you can still strop the blade with a leather belt. A good compromise is to carry a small, fine whetstone and a rod, then to use the leather belt for field stropping.

Ceramic Rods

Ceramic rods are a honing device and are used to finely dress the blades for burrs before stropping. They are not a necessity, but a small, pencil-size rod will take up little room in your kit. In any case, these rods, whether at home or in the wild, will allow you to obtain a very keen edge both in season and during routine maintenance in the off seasons.

Honing with a ceramic rod is just like honing with a whetstone, but the contact surface is much smaller because of the round rod. Ceramic rods are best used to remove any burr created during the sharpening process, but you can use them as a honing device without sharpening if the knife is cared for properly.

Stropping

Stropping refers to the buffing of the blade and is the final process in making a keen cutting edge. If you don't let your knife go too long without a proper sharpening, stropping alone can often bring the edge back very quickly. In the field, a good leather belt will work as a strop. When stropping, you will actually be pulling the blade in the opposite direction as you would with a stone or rod. A good practice is to find the angle of grind, then hold the knife itself at a 45° angle to the strop, drawing it toward you with the blade edge away from you.

SAWS

Another essential cutting tool for your kit is the **saw**. As with knives, a wide variety of saws is available, and they have many important uses.

FOLDING SAWS

There are many types of folding saws on the market today, and these are great tools for you to carry into the woods as they are lightweight, compact, and relatively inexpensive. Using a saw is always safer than swinging an axe, and unless you are very skilled with an axe, a saw will be more precise as well. You can avoid a lot of the batoning process when making notches if you have a saw handy, and for trimming and limbing this tool is hard to beat.

> **BUSHCRAFT TIP**
>
> You can split wood fairly easily using a saw: Take a dry branch, approximately wrist size in diameter, and make a stop cut about halfway through the material. Then smack the piece on an anvil or stump with the stop cut perpendicular to the ground. This should split the branch from the stop cut forward in half.

Many brands of folding saws are on the market, but in my experience the Bahco Laplander is the best saw on the market for bushcraft, and at about $30 is very affordable. My own saw is more than six years old and is still going strong.

BOW SAWS (FRAME SAWS)

The terms *bow saw*, *buck saw*, and *frame saw* are fairly synonymous; each is a single blade with a frame to hold it rigid. The type I choose to carry is a bow saw. This is a tubular metal frame in a "D" shape with a blade connected to the two ends. They come in sizes from 12–30" and have blades made for many tasks, such as cutting green wood, rough cutting dry wood, or cutting metal. Only carry a bow saw if you are planning a longer excursion (a week or more) into an area where you may need to process larger wood. The power of a good bow saw should not be underestimated; it can make short work of a downed tree and quickly create a large firewood pile. I choose to carry a 20" bow saw, as I like my larger tools to be about the length of my bedroll, or about the length of my armpit to my palm. A frame added to a 20" blade makes the saw about 23–24" overall. A bow saw is a great companion to an axe when felling trees; it's well adapted to make the felling cut, it's great for limbing, and it's the best tool for cutting wood to firewood length once a tree is cut or deadwood is found.

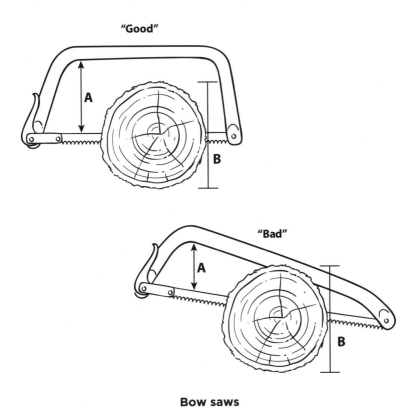

Bow saws

Bow Saw Frame Types

There are many shapes of bow saws, from a basic "D"-style design to an almost triangular shape. Here is the thing to remember about frame saws in general: They are only capable of making a cut as deep as the frame is high. Any angle in the frame will decrease the length of stroke when cutting wood larger in diameter than the height of the saw frame. There are also take-down or folding bow saws on the market, made of both wood and metal, but I have never been a big believer in moving parts or taking things apart in the woods. A metal tube is about as indestructible as you can get.

SAW SAFETY

Always keep blades of bow saws covered when not in use. The easiest method for this is to remove the blade at one end of the frame, place —" PVC over the blade, then lock it back into the frame. When sawing wood, always place your free hand through the frame to ensure that the saw cannot jump from the cut or cause injury. When using the saw, place your free hand (the one through the frame) on the off fall side. By applying pressure, you will open the gap (or kerf) caused by the blade; this will keep the saw from sticking as it gets deeper in the wood. Saws can make a nasty jagged cut if mishandled, so be deliberate, be safe, and take your time.

SAW CARE

The blade of your saw may be subject to wear and/or damage from rust. Keep it oiled with the same lubricants you use for your knife and other metal tools. The teeth of your blade are offset, creating the kerf (the space in the cut where wood has been removed); the amount of offset dictates the width of the kerf. As you use the blade, this offset will reduce (and the kerf along with it), causing the blade to bind, or stick, when cutting. Resetting the teeth is more complicated and time-consuming than you probably want to deal with. It is generally cheaper to replace the blade; always carry a spare.

However, if you're in the field for a long time, you may need a way of resetting the teeth. You can accomplish this chore in two ways:

1. Use a small set of pliers (possibly a multi-tool or set in your trapping gear) to gently bend every other tooth outward, making sure every alternate one is pushed a bit in the opposite direction.

2. Remove the blade, lay it down on a stump or tree anvil, and gently tap a nail with your axe, moving every other tooth a bit. Then flip the blade and repeat on the other side. This procedure will in no way be exact, but in an emergency it works better than nothing. You can buy commercial tooth-setting tools, but that is another piece of gear to carry and it's not necessary, as the blades will last a long time before needing to be replaced or reset.

Always remember to replace your blade cover when you're finished using your saw.

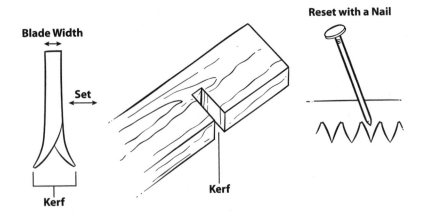

Reset with a Nail

Blade Width

Set

Kerf

Kerf

Saw kerf and set

AXES

There are many types of axes, handles, and head weights available to the woodsman today, and many are meant for a specific purpose. What you need to consider as the tramping solitary bushcrafter is what needs your axe must fulfill, what types of wood are most commonly found in your area, and how much weight you are willing to carry. The larger the axe, the safer it will be to handle; it will take less inertia to remove material and will require a lighter, more controlled swing. We'll first discuss the different kinds of axes and then learn more about selection and use.

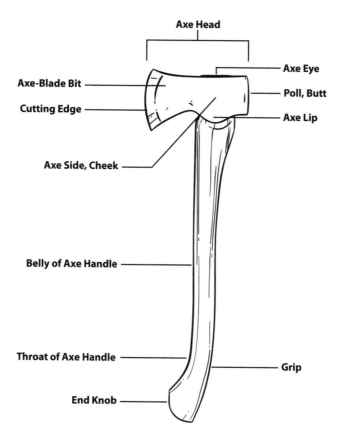

The parts of the axe

TOMAHAWKS

Many of our forefathers carried the belt axe or hatchet as an everyday item; many also carried the **tomahawk** in lieu of a hatchet. A tomahawk differs from a belt axe mainly in that its handle can be easily removed, making it a hand tool that can be used for other tasks as well as chopping. The handle of a true tomahawk is generally thin and straight, as compared to the axe or hatchet handles, which have a slight curve. Both handles are made of good hardwood such as hickory, but the tomahawk handle is held in place largely by pressure; the handle is tapered and threaded through the head from the top. The tapering keeps the handle from going completely through the head "eye" of the tomahawk, but because it is not fastened into place, it can be easily removed or replaced if desired or if broken.

While the romantic stories about tomahawk fights along the frontier may be true, this was not the initial purpose of the tool. The tomahawk was an early multi-tool and could be used for processing smaller firewood around camp. With the head removed from the handle, it makes an excellent scraping and skinning tool and can also be used as a wedge for splitting logs. For these reasons, the tomahawk is better to carry than a small belt axe, if the purpose of your journey is working a trap line or processing skins.

BELT AXES (HATCHETS)

Belt axes, also known as crafting axes or hatchets, have been a staple from the early days along the American frontier; even every Boy Scout had a hatchet within his kit. Belt axes come in many patterns, and hatchets do as well. The main criteria for any of these are similar to a knife: You want the head to be high-carbon steel and hand forged if possible. Always choose a wooden handle so that emergency replacement is possible while afield. Beyond these recommendations, size, weight, and shape are matters of personal preference. Any axe or hatchet with a handle length of less than 16" and a head of less than 2 pounds can be hung on the belt or attached to the body without becoming overly cumbersome.

CHOOSING A LARGER AXE

Axes are also available in many patterns, as well as weights and handle lengths. The decision to carry an axe large enough that you must attach it to a pack or frame must be justified by the type of work to be done around the camp and on the trail. An axe with a handle length that spans from your armpit to your palm is a good felling axe. You'll only need this size if it's necessary to fell larger-diameter trees. (Large trees, for purposes of this book, include timbers large enough to be considered structural, or 8" in diameter and larger.) For smaller tasks than these, an axe somewhere in between the size of a felling axe or belt axe will work nicely and will be very useful for other camp tasks. The hunter's variety of axe, with handles from 15–18", is about the best compromise for an all-around axe. As for the brands or types of axes that suit the woodsman best, the Swedish axe makers are the best. I have never had an S.A. Wetterlings brand or Gränsfors Bruk fail me in the field.

GRINDS

When selecting any axe, the blade grind depends on its intended use. A more convex grind will be a great splitter for dry wood, but it may not penetrate damp or frozen wood as well and will demand more of your energy. A convex grind is not good for finer tasks, such as pointing stakes and uprights or cutting notches into logs. A more Scandinavian "Scandi" type of grind is a good all-around grind both for splitting firewood and for construction. Most of these Swedish-type axes have a slight secondary bevel on the face of the bit to create the actual cutting edge.

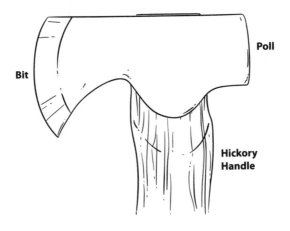

Poll

Bit

Hickory
Handle

Scandinavian axe head

SAFE HANDLING AND USE

One of the marks of skilled woodsman is how he handles and cares for his tools. It is important to *always* keep a proper mask on any axe or hatchet not in use. Always have a durable and safe mask available, or be ready to make one at a moment's notice. Never lay your axe on the ground; it could become a tripping hazard. Instead, lean it head-down against a tree or return it to your pack system. When preparing to wield an axe, just as with a knife, you should ensure a clear area—not only clear of others but also of anything that might entangle your axe during the swing or deflect it from an even arc. Always ensure that wherever your axe will strike, a glancing blow or miscalculated strike will not injure you or damage your axe by hitting rock or soil. It is good practice when splitting wood to use an anvil, whether it be larger wood stumps or bucked stubs. You can also create an anvil by notching a downed log with a large log cabin notch to give yourself a flat surface.

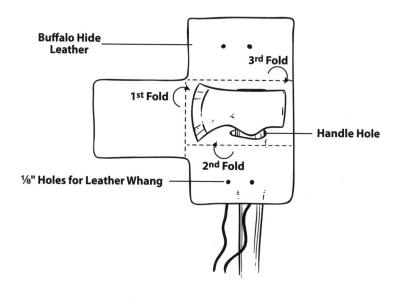

Buffalo Hide Leather

3rd Fold

1st Fold

Handle Hole

⅛" Holes for Leather Whang

2nd Fold

Axe mask

SPLITTING FIREWOOD

If possible, you should split firewood while kneeling so as to eliminate travel of the axe if you miss the log. This will clear your legs of possible contact and keep you in a much safer position than standing. To accomplish this, kneel in front of the anvil and adjust your position so that when the axe head is in the middle of the anvil, your arms are outstretched. In this position, the axe may strike the ground (although this isn't desired), but it can never swing into your legs or feet. Never use a knife for a job that can be accomplished by an axe, but be mindful that the smaller your firewood becomes, the more dangerous it becomes to process with a heavy implement.

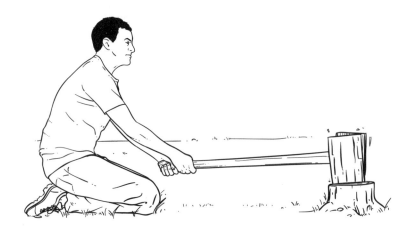

Safe wood-splitting position

Another way to split a plank of wood is to lay it horizontally on the anvil instead of vertically. This will create a smaller margin for a miss and allow easy splitting to kindling size. Remember when splitting any wood that it will tend to fly left or right of the anvil; these areas should be cleared of persons or gear before starting. Once you have processed the wood to smaller than wrist-size pieces, you can use a compound anvil for final splitting of longer pieces. Place the desired piece onto the anvil horizontally; once you've made the strike and the axe has penetrated through the wood into the anvil, leave the axe stationary and pull the wood to one side to complete the split.

PROCESSING FIREWOOD

You should be able to process an 8" diameter log that is approximately 12" long into 88 pieces of kindling if necessary, or into any derivative that is needed from that. Use pieces at least 2" in diameter for fuel sources, and pieces no bigger than large #2 pencils as kindling. Remember that harder and green woods will burn longer, but softer deadwood will take flame faster, so a combination may be necessary for a good fire lay, depending on your conditions.

FELLING

Felling a tree can have an effect on the environment, so it should not be done lightly. Always use deadwood for any construction and smaller saplings when you can. If it's necessary to fell a tree, consider the following before you proceed:

1. Select the smallest available tree that will meet the needs you have.
2. Ensure that the safe zone is clear of any gear or obstructions. (This includes other trees that may affect the fall of the intended tree. A tree hung halfway down in another tree top presents a whole other set of issues.)
3. Ensure that you have a good escape route from the area behind where the tree will hinge.

JUDGING THE HEIGHT OF A TREE

To understand the safe area you must create before felling a tree, you need to know how tall the tree is so you know how much area is needed. To accomplish this, you can use your compass inclinometer. Move away from the tree until aiming the compass at the top shows a 45° angle on the inclinometer. At this point, the distance you are away from the tree will be approximately equal to its height.

BUSHCRAFT TIP

If you don't have a compass, use any measuring device. I generally burn marks into the back of my axe handle at 1" increments. Take a measurement from the base of the tree, and tie a cord at a convenient height, such as 5'. Step away from the tree until you can capture that 5' of height within the 1" mark on your axe. At this point, look up at the top of the tree and figure how many marks on the axe the tree is tall, and then multiply that by 5' to get an approximate height of the tree.

SAFE ZONE

Felling large trees should be attempted only by the experienced bushcrafter, as it can be dangerous. To choose trees of load-bearing grade that are still fairly safe, use the "reach around test." Hug the tree you have selected, and if you can touch your left shoulder with your right hand, or vice versa, it is of a safe size to tackle alone or without a lot of experience. Always try to fell on level ground without large rocks or other levering points in the path of the falling tree. Check the safe zone—an area 180° in the direction of the intended felling—to be sure all personnel and equipment are clear.

FELLING CUTS

To fell a tree, assume a position for chopping to one side of the tree—never behind it—and a full axe length away. Check to ensure that you have an escape route and have cleared the area of entanglements, etc.

Felling a tree requires that you make two cuts to create a hinge for the tree to fall and not shear. (If the tree shears it can kick backward, possibly causing injury.) The first cut is made on the front of the tree in the direction of the intended felling, and is called the undercut or front notch. This will be a notch that is flat or perpendicular at the bottom and is at a 45° angle at the top. This cut should be about as high as half the diameter of the tree, and cut a bit more than one-third of the way through the tree. The second cut, which is made to the backside of the tree opposite the felling direction, is called the felling cut. It is made with either a saw or axe, and is set up to have the apex of any angled cut approximately 2" above the front cut apex. This will create a hinge that makes the tree fall forward. This cut should only be about one-third the diameter of the tree, as to leave a hinge. Wedges are used to ease momentum of the tree toward the felling cut.

Wood harvesting with hand tools

LIMBING

After a tree has been cut down, or if you wish to process a **deadfall** tree, you will need to limb it (that is, trim off the limbs), either for further processing or to collect firewood. When limbing a tree, always stand on the opposite side of the trunk from the limb you intend to cut. That way, the axe can never strike you. To limb a tree that is lying on the ground, always cut from the back of the limb's connection to the tree, not into the crotch or apex of the connection. Splitting into the crotch will often cause the tree to split and not clean-cut the branch.

BUCKING AND NOTCHING

Cutting logs for splitting ("bucking") or notching them with an axe so they can be used in construction is usually done, as with a saw, by jacking by tripod. (Jacking by tripod means using a tripod to support the area to be cut so that you have a free hanging end of the log or branch, and so that the blade doesn't stick in the cut.) When bucking logs with an axe, use a V notch and roll the log to make four cuts, completing the separation. When cutting a notch in the log, you should actually stand on top of the log to make your cuts, if possible. If the log diameter is too small to stand on comfortably, stand opposite to the side you are cutting. Never make the cut on top of the log, but always on the sides to avoid errant glances that could cause injury.

BATONING THE AXE

For purposes of making slats, planks, or shingles, fashion a large baton so you can use the blade of the axe in place of a **froe** (a froe is a flat metal cutting blade attached to a handle; it's used with a baton to make thin splits of flat plank wood when making shingles). As with the tomahawk head, this will allow you to use the axe head in a more controlled fashion as a wedge for splitting off these items from a heavily grained hardwood or cedar.

AXE CARE AND SHARPENING

As with any tool, your axe needs tender loving care to remain at peak efficiency. This includes storage, maintenance, and blade sharpening. Here are some basics of axe care.

HANDLE CARE

When you purchase an axe, pay particular attention to the handle's grain. Handles should be made of hickory and have a straight grain running the length of the handle with no run-outs to the outer edges. (Run-outs can cause the handle to split during use.) There should be no knots within the handle. Sapwood handles are better than hardwood, but a mix of both is okay. Treat your handle with linseed oil to seal it after use, as the finish will wear and it will be susceptible to drying out and possibly cracking. How often you do this depends on humidity, temperature, and use.

AXE HEAD

Caring for the head of your axe is no different than caring for any other high-carbon tool. It will rust, so it must be kept lubricated. Again, I generally use olive oil for this purpose (although I would rarely use my axe for any food processing); it keeps things consistent in caring for all my tools and metal gear.

SHARPENING

Just as with a knife, there are several tools to use when sharpening or honing an axe. A Carborundum stone with medium and fine grit sides will take care of 95 percent of your needs, and you can carry a small one in the field. Lansky makes a tool called the puck that is a fine and medium two-sided sharpening tool, about the size of a hockey puck. It works very well. As with whetstones, I prefer to use water and not oil as a lubricant for the puck. When using this type of stone, make circular strokes to sharpen the blade, attending to both sides evenly, as with a knife. If your axe gets a bad nick from a missed swing or glance, you may need a fine mill file to remove the nick. Then sharpen it with the stone.

When using a file, place the axe in a stable position and push the file with the angle of the grind against and into the blade, or away from it, depending on your preference. To remove these nicks or dings, slow even strokes will be both safe and accurate. Stropping an axe is unnecessary, as a fine stone will make your cutting edge plenty keen. As with knives, grind on axes varies, and following the existing angle is best.

ALWAYS CARRY WEDGES

Wedges are of great use in the woods for many tasks, but we will discuss just a few here. You can make them from wood, but it is highly recommended that you carry at least two prefabricated ones. Wedges made from ABS plastic materials are cheap and lightweight; they can be easily carried and can be a lifesaver.

WEDGES FOR FELLING

Once you make a felling cut and the tree starts to fall in the intended direction, place a good wedge into the felling cut and tap it in with the blunt end (the "hammer pole") of the axe. Of course this should be done with care and never from directly behind the tree.

WEDGES FOR LOG SPLITTING

When splitting a complete log, after you make the initial splitting cut use several wedges to help split the log along its axis. Baton the wedges into the crack successively as the log begins to split.

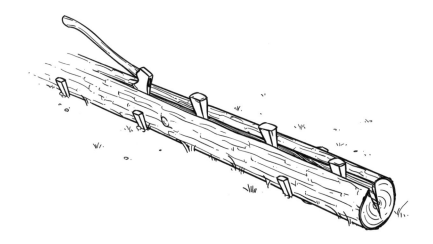

Wedges for log splitting

WEDGES TO FREE YOUR KNIFE

At times while batoning or splitting wood with a knife, you will get your blade stuck in the piece being split. If this happens, place a wedge into the initial split, and drive it in by baton to open the slit and free your blade.

TIPS AND TRICKS FOR YOUR TOOLS

1. Make an easy, packable sharpening board by attaching 1200 grit wet/dry sandpaper to a paint stick, using double-sided carpet tape.
2. If you break the handle of your axe and need to remove it for replacement, the best way to do this is by burning it out. Bury the actual cutting edge up to the cheek in dirt; then build a small fire around the eye to remove the old handle material without removing the temper from the cutting blade.

3. If your knife does not have a 90° spine capable of removing material from your ferrocerium rod, you can use a mill file and vise to carefully remove material and square the spine.

4. To quickly add a protective patina to your high-carbon blade that will help protect it from rust, use the juice from green-black walnut hulls; apply it liberally to the blade and leave it to set for two hours. This will give you a nice black patina. Then oil and store.

5. To make a safety cover for the cutting blade of your bow saw, cut a poplar sapling in the spring and split the bark lengthwise. Remove the bark from the wood, place around your blade, and let dry.

— Chapter 3 —
ROPE, CORDAGE,
Webbings, and Knots

"It is extraordinary how little the average individual knows about the art of making even the simplest knots."
—R.M. ABRAHAM, *WINTER NIGHTS ENTERTAINMENTS*, 1932

You must carry cordage as one of the main elements of your kit because of its usefulness in creating other items. You must also carry it because it's difficult to create in large quantity with natural material, and doing so would take a lot of time. Cordage is useful for making fire, lashings, and bindings and is helpful in trapping, fishing, and a host of other things. Therefore, it is important for you to take a close look at the cordage you choose to carry within your kit. Just like all the other elements of the Five Cs, it must be capable of a multitude of tasks. While cord and rope are actually synonymous terms, for sake of this book we will identify cordage as having a diameter less than ¼", and rope as anything above ¼" that is made from multiple fibers, whether they are natural or synthetic.

CORDS

Some cords, such as Military 550 cord (**parachute cord**), have an outer sheath called a mantle. This is a woven sheath, generally of poly material, that covers inner strands or cords. In the case of true 550 cords, there are seven strands inside the mantle. The 550 cords are popular within the camping realm because most survival-type manuals mention this cord; they do so because many of the older survival manuals were largely based on military doctrines, and the military had plenty of 550 cord. In earlier times, ropes and cords were made of natural materials such as **hemp**, cotton, jute, or sisal.

There are many types of cord available for you to use in the bush, but I find mariner's tarred twisted nylon twine to be superior cordage to anything else available today. It is made of three fibers of synthetic material that are woven together. It comes in strengths of line tests from about 80# test to over 500# test (these numbers refer to the twine's tensile strength) in a thin diameter and useful package. The biggest fault of the traditional para cord (550) is that it's really only useful in its original state. Once the mantle is removed, the seven inner strands tend to split apart and fray easily. This makes it difficult to extend the amount of cordage you have by breaking it down, or reducing the diameter to meet the need at hand. Para cord works well for making improvised fishing lures and lillian for cane poles (the lillian is an attachment braid on the end of a tenkara rod; see Chapter 10). Tarred mariner's line, however, breaks down easily to three smaller fibers, has a tar coating that protects it from UV rays, and binds well to itself when using it for lashings or bindings. I generally carry a 1# roll of two different sizes: #12 and #36. The #12 is great for net-making and fishing, while the #36 works for any heavy lashings and bindings or to include tarp guy lines.

ROPE

Unlike cord, I prefer my rope to be of a natural material such as hemp. The main reason for this is its flammability, which aids in fire-making and when creating a bird's nest (discussed later). Rope can be used for a number of things, such as improvised pack and bedroll straps. It can be worn as a belt for your outermost garments to keep your sheath knife and belt pouch readily available without your having to fumble under your coat or blanket shirt. You can also use rope for many camp chores, such as suspending game animals for processing, pulling tent stakes, hanging a hammock, or improvising a windlass to move a heavy object. I recommend carrying about two ropes 12' in length and one rope 25' in length at all times when tramping alone.

WEBBING

Tubular webbing is used for climbing, so it has a very high tensile strength to prevent breakage. It has some advantages over rope in that it weighs less, takes up less room, and has a higher tensile strength. When making improvised straps and such from this material, you'll find it much more comfortable over distance than rope. Because webbing is flat, you'll be able to carry more of it. Because webbing takes up less room than rope (generally), I recommend two 20' sections and a 50' section if room and weight allow. This material will do anything rope will do—and a bit better in most cases, other than help with fire-starting. You can always carry a bit of both, as I do.

MULE TAPE

Mule tape is a mantle with no inner strands and is used by electricians. It has a very high tensile strength relative to its size, and you can carry 100' without adding more than a pound or so to your pack.

Mors Kochanski, Boreal bushcraft instructor and a well-known Canadian writer, is a big believer in this product, and I respect his opinion. However, like all other components of your kit, environment is a very important consideration. In the eastern woodlands, there are so many briars, cat claws, and thorns in general that mantle-type cord or rope is not feasible because of the fraying of the fibers and weaves over time. However, if your environment allows it, it is great for all things of which a heavier rope would be capable.

MAKING NATURAL CORDAGE

To make natural cord, first you must know the correct material to use for this purpose. It must be fairly strong, depending on its application, and it must be available during all four seasons. There are many plants and trees that will make natural cord in the eastern woodlands. To make a single cord from natural material of passable strength, you only need to look as far as vines or the roots of spruce trees on the ground. Some of these can be relatively strong, and it is best to test materials in your area before the need arises by harvesting a section and attempting to tie an overhand knot in the cord. If doing this breaks the cord, it may not be viable for some tasks, but if you can make three or four wraps around your finger and it does not split or break, it may be passable for some applications.

REVERSE-WRAP TWO-PLY CORDAGE

To make this type of cord in the eastern woodland, the best material will be the inner barks of the shagbark hickory or the tulip tree (yellow poplar). Other options for plant fibers outside the eastern woodland are yucca and nettle, as well as dogbane. Yellow poplar is by far the easiest and will make a good strong cord for most applications in any diameter needed. Recently fallen or dead fallen poplar is the least desirable cordage material but will be the easiest to harvest. Pry the edge of this bark with a knife and peel it off; it should come off in long strips depending on the branch or tree. Then remove the outer bark to get to the inner bark fibers. To do this, work the piece around a rough-barked sapling or a rope; this will loosen and remove the outer bark. Once the fibers are obtained, you need to process them further into smaller strands, then into groups of strands to obtain the desired diameter of cord.

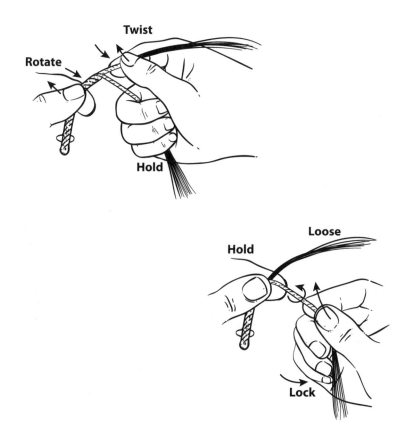

How to make cordage

When you are ready to begin, separate the strands into two separate bundles. Holding both bundles at the same time but keeping them separate, twist them one at a time in the same direction.

After this, pinch both bundles together and twist both bundles in the opposite direction (that is, they are reverse wrapped and twisted first one way then against themselves the other), and then repeat the entire process until finished. It is best to start with bundles of two different lengths so that you can splice another bundle into the cord to add length. Do this only on one side at a time, never at the same time. When you reach approximately 1" from the end of the shortest bundle, add another bundle on that side, twisting it with the tail and making it one bundle. Then, continue to reverse wrap as normal until the splice is within the cord. If a stronger cord is desired, you can always use two cords fully processed, and cord them together with the same process. This will give you roughly two-thirds the original strength of a single strand the same diameter. This same technique can be used with cords such as mariner's tarred twisted nylon twine to create a stronger cord as well.

BASIC AND USEFUL CAMP KNOTS

Knots are the basis of all lashings and bindings, as well as essential for securing anything from a load to a toggle. We use knots in life every day, and there are hundreds to choose from. Practice knots often until you've mastered them; you should be able to tie them behind your back and blindfolded so that you can do them without thinking if needed! Whether you're tying down gear to a frame or building a shelter, the use of knots, lashings, and bindings is a critical skill. Many knots will allow you to recover cords that may otherwise need to be cut, and this will conserve an important resource. Proper lashings can mean the difference in a shelter that stands a storm or one that collapses under the weight of snow, and a pack frame that lasts for years or breaks three miles into a weekend tramp.

Of the hundreds of knots available, this section only covers a few that I consider essential for bushcraft, as well as the importance of cord recovery to conserve a resource. We will discuss three basic types of knots: slipknots, binding knots, and static knots. Slipknots, as the word implies, tighten with the slippage of one line though a loop or loops in another. Binding knots tighten by friction of rope on rope. Static knots are standalone knots and do not require further action to function as a knot.

STOP KNOT

A stop knot is a simple overhand knot used at the end of a line that will keep the rope from slipping. The knot works well with any other knot as a security measure. Generally, you want this simple overhand knot to have some tail beyond the knot itself. With any line or knot, you should tie a simple overhand stop knot on the tag end to ensure that if a knot does slip, it will not come undone. The stop knot will keep the line from slipping completely through.

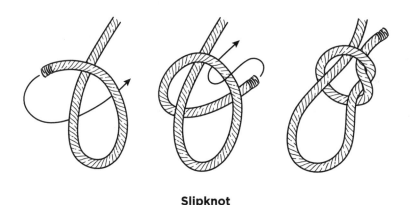

Slipknot

BOWLINE KNOT

The bowline knot (pronounced BO-lin) is one of the four basic mariner's knots. This knot is a standalone knot, and is also a main knot used in rescue operations. This knot will retain two-thirds of the line's tensile strength even under load and is ideal for putting a static loop at the end of any line. The single downside of this knot is its tendency to slide or come undone under a heavy load, depending on the cord used to make it. However, this can be easily circumvented with a stop knot on the tail.

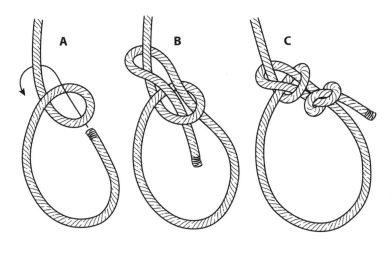

Bowline knot

The bowline knot is best for any end-of-the-line application where you need a loop to pass the line through and tighten around an object, such as the ridgeline of a shelter. This knot will be easy enough to remove even if great stress is placed on the line. It is useful for incorporation with other knots, such as the lark's head, for tarp tie-out lines, and for toggles at the end of a line as well.

LARK'S HEAD KNOT

This knot is a self tightening–style knot that can be used in a variety of situations, for everything from attaching toggles with a stop knot to attaching one line to another for the purpose of hanging something from a toggle. The lark's head knot is formed by two simple loops. However, this knot will slip if pulled under a very heavy load side to side (unlike the prusik knot). It's great for tarp adjustment lines, especially when using two ropes of different diameters, with the lark's head being the smaller cord. I consider this the second most versatile knot for use in the woods.

Lark's head knot

JAM KNOT

The jam knot is a slipknot that, when used in conjunction with a stop knot, jams a loop of line to tighten around an object. This knot is easily released by pulling the tail on the stop knot portion of the line. This is one of the most useful knots for its adaptability.

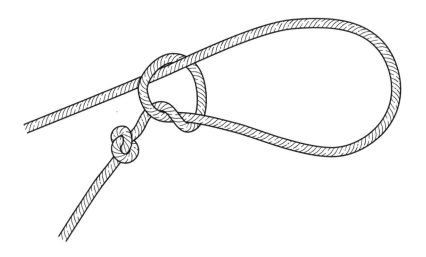

Jam knot

TRUCKER'S HITCH

A combination of two slipknots, this knot is used for putting a line under tension and keeping it taut. It can be used for any application when a line must be drawn tight but will still easily release for adjustment or recovery.

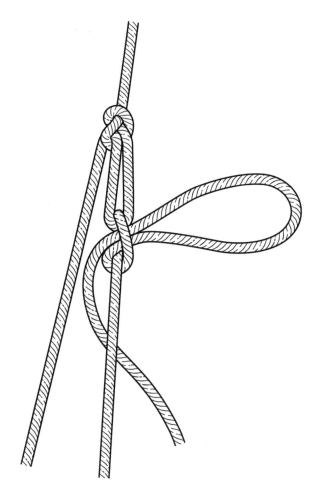

Trucker's hitch

PRUSIK KNOT

The prusik knot is used to attach a loop of line to another line of larger diameter. The loop will tighten when tension is placed on it, making it tight on the larger line. This is a load-bearing knot that is used for ascending a rope or managing a rope crossing in swift water, as it will easily slide forward or up the rope, but self-tightens again under friction. This is also a knot with which to maintain a taut line connected to a tie-out point for tarps and shelters.

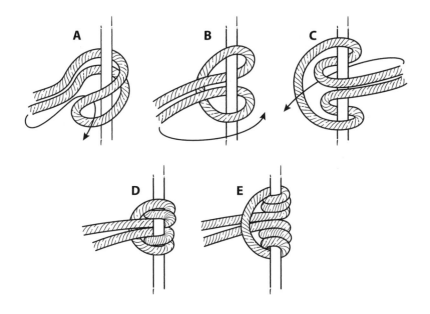

Prusik knot

FISHERMAN'S KNOT

These knots are simple overhand knots used to create a loop of line from a single piece. This is a slipknot as well and tightens against the opposite knot when pulled, but it can be loosened easily by pulling on the tails. The loops are very useful in prusik and lark's head configurations.

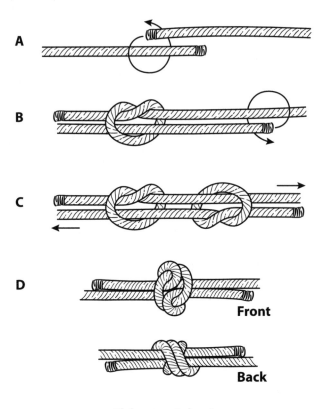

A

B

C

D

Front

Back

Fisherman's knot

TIMBER HITCH

Timber hitches are friction knots. A timber hitch will bind against itself under pressure, and is used in applications of lashings, bow strings, ridgelines, etc.

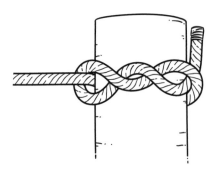

Timber hitch

CLOVE HITCH

This knot is also one of the four main mariner's knots, and is very useful if you need to adjust the line after setting. The knot will loosen when either end of the rope is pushed toward the knot, but it is more difficult to loosen in smaller-diameter cords. It is a good ending knot for lashings, as it makes cord recovery possible.

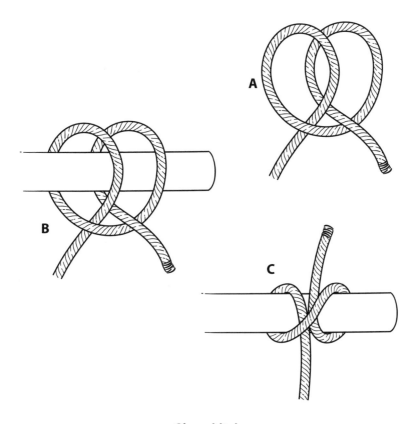

Clove hitch

LASHINGS, BINDINGS, AND TOGGLES

LASHINGS

Lashings are used in constructing objects from the landscape that will be under some load or are meant to support something else. Tripods, pack frames, camp furniture, and A-frame shelter supports all require lashings to make them strong. For basic bushcraft, you will need to understand the straight or shear lash and the diagonal or cross lash. Shear lashings are used when two objects are tied side by side and then separated, causing the lashing to tighten further. A diagonal lash is used with sticks that cross each other while being lashed, like the top of a Roycroft pack frame.

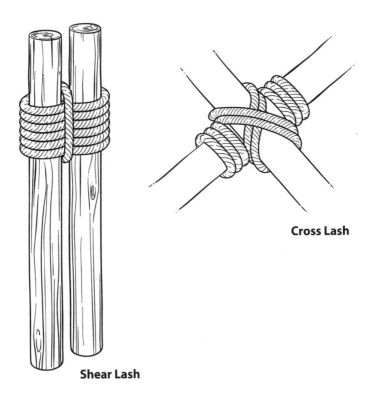

Cross Lash

Shear Lash

Shear lashing and diagonal lashing

BINDINGS

Bindings are used to keep something from separating or coming apart. You use a binding, for example, to wrap the end of a cut rope to keep the rope end from further fraying. You may also use a binding to haft something, such as a knife blade or arrow point, to a handle. Sometimes bindings are used in conjunction with adhesives and sometimes not, depending on application.

TOGGLES

Toggles are among the most useful items in the woodsman's box of knowledge. They can be used for almost any application, from sheltering to cooking to trapping, or even packing and carrying gear. A toggle is a simple wood stick or dowel (size dependent on need), which is connected to a line by a knot. This can be used as a simple attachment point that is easily moved or removed, and will be load bearing if needed.

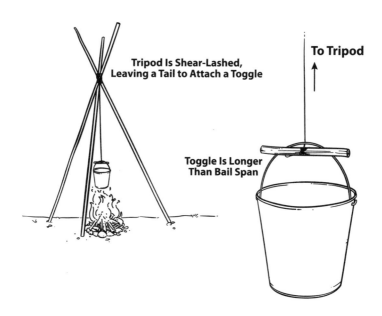

Tripod toggle setup

TIPS AND TRICKS FOR ROPE AND CORDAGE

1. Toggles in rope tied with a lark's head knot and a jam knot are great for hanging gear such as haversacks, packs, and even guns to keep them off the ground.

2. Ropes made of natural fiber such as cotton are great for use as a charred slow match. Place a section into tubing such as copper, light a small amount of exposed end, and then blow it out to char the material. You can then re-light the match easily with ferrocerium rod or flint and steel to create a large ember. By feeding the rope up through the tube, you can extend its burn time. Use about 12" of ⅜–½" rope and a similar length of 6" copper or brass tubing. To put the ember out, just draw the burning end back into the tube.

3. To make cordage from an animal's rawhide, insert your knife into a section of a stump and thinly slice the hide in a circular fashion. The knife is stationary in the stump and the hide is drawn toward the blade to make the cut. This will give you much longer single cords than trying to cut a piece along the length of hide.

4. Remember that nylon-based cords, such as parachute cord, will melt if burned. By using only the outer mantle of this cord and melting it, you can make an emergency adhesive or patch for small holes, in items such as containers.

5. Ensure that any natural cordage is not stored wet; this will cause mildew and break down the fibers.

— Chapter 4 —
CONTAINERS
and Cooking Tools

"The simpler the outfit, the more skill it takes to manage it, and the more pleasure one gets in his achievements."
—HORACE KEPHART, *CAMP COOKERY*, 1910

In every good kit you'll find items for heating water, cooking foods, and making medicinal teas and decoctions. There are many types of containers and cooking apparatuses from which you can choose, and the modern age of ultralight camping gives you even more options than before. Choosing bottles, cups, pots, and pans that are made from the right material is an important decision and should reflect your needs in the bush. Therefore, it is crucial to know the different cookware materials before you make any purchases or venture into the wild.

From the mid-nineteenth to the early twentieth century, the majority of cookware carried afoot was made of aluminum or steel. Earlier explorers used tin, copper, and cast-iron cooking tools as well. Modern technology has produced a wide variety of stainless steel products from which you can choose, as well as superlight titanium cookware. (Indeed, you can purchase cookware that weighs next to nothing; an entire set of modern cookware has about the same weight as a single object made 100 years ago!) However, lightweight materials do not wear well over time. I have found that while titanium is great for quick heating, it is also very susceptible to warping under direct flame. It may be great if you're going to cook with a camp stove, but for the real bushman who wants his victuals cooked over an open flame, it falls short of the mark.

Stainless steel is strong and resilient, holds heat well, and cooks efficiently when lubricated with oil. It does have one downside: It is very heavy compared to titanium and aluminum. Aluminum is one of the best materials for resilience, heat transfer, and weight. There was much controversy in the 1960s and 1970s surrounding aluminum cookware and products, when scientists feared a link between aluminum and Alzheimer's disease. Recent studies have failed to confirm this, however. Today, anodized aluminums are available that are coated to remove direct contact with foods and liquids during heating and cooking. Steel, stainless steel, and anodized aluminum are all passable choices, depending on your personal taste and preference, but stainless steel is the winner for sheer durability.

WATER BOTTLES/CANTEENS

Containers are crucial to any kit; they are one of the Five Cs because of the difficulty of making a container for water from natural materials in the wild. It's key that you have the ability to disinfect water by heating it; as well, rapid rewarming by heated liquids can be a lifesaver should you become hypothermic. Water bottles are a new item when it comes to woodland tramping. In the days of Nessmuk and Kephart, canteens were available but were rarely mentioned as an everyday carry. Today we're more familiar with waterborne pathogens and thus concerned with the quality of our water containers. Whatever the case, you must ensure the quality of water you drink.

Water bottles that are plastic are a waste of time and money. Any container you choose to carry must be capable of withstanding direct flame. The CDC and the Wilderness Medical Society agree that the *only* 100 percent sure way to disinfect water for safe consumption is to boil it. At normal altitudes of less than 5,000 feet, once the water comes to a rolling boil, that is enough contact time under heat to kill all live waterborne threats. To accomplish this, you must have a metal vessel. I recommend a stainless steel water bottle that holds at least 32 ounces. This means you must boil water four times per day to maintain normal body function. Smaller bottles mean more boiling, and larger bottles become a weight issue if carried full. There are many good water bottles on the market today, but ensure that the one you buy is of one-piece construction for durability in the fire.

There are very few high-quality metal canteens on the market. The only stainless steel canteen I know of is carried by Self Reliance Outfitters and comes with a cup and stove stand. The aluminum canteens on the market are not anodized, nor are they as durable as stainless steel.

You can use a toggle and string to suspend a water bottle or canteen over the fire or to remove it when heating is completed. To accomplish this, tie the toggle with a clove hitch off center a bit. This will allow the toggle to pivot into place and out of place easily when not under tension, but lock into the shoulders of the bottle when suspended.

CUPS

Cups are available in all the same materials as bottles, and many are made to nest on the bottom of the bottle itself. Some cups are available with a stove stand. Any cup you carry is a personal choice. Many woodsmen of the past considered their cup to have special meaning; their cups would help "smooth it" in the woods. Noggins or **kuksas** are cups generally made from wood, although there are composite and ABS plastic versions available as well. Original Swedish kuksas were made of sturdy, olive green plastic. Some metal cups have measurement markers either engraved or indented in them, which makes them a good choice for camp cookery.

Canteen cups are mainly made of stainless steel, but handle configurations will vary from a folding single strap handle to butterfly-type handles. Single strap handles make the cup more stable on the ground, and they can be easily modified by adding "D" rings on the strap. This will make it possible to add a stick for a longer handle, to make cooking more enjoyable (this is very similar to the Swedish cook sets). Another easy modification to your cup is to drill holes just under the rim perpendicular to the handles and approximately ⅛" in diameter. This will allow you to use a fish mouth spreader as a bail for the cup, making it possible to employ it as a hanging pot. Many lids are available as well for cups (both regular style and canteen cups) to make them more versatile cook pots. A new technological improvement over the U.S. Canteen Cup Stove ring for both bottles and canteens is the stainless steel cook stove. This stove nests under the cup, which allows you to use **Trangia** or other alcohol stoves for heating and cooking in place of fire. (This is especially efficient if you're stopped briefly at a campsite, or if open fire is an environmental issue.) These items are also available from Self Reliance Outfitters.

"D" Rings Added to Folding Handle Enable Stick to Be Added for Extended Cooking Reach

U.S. Canteen Cup

How to modify a canteen cup

POTS

Bush pots and cook sets were among the most common items carried by woodsmen of the past, and they're just as important now. These items sometimes nest so that several pieces can be carried in one space within the pack. In his book *Camping and Woodcraft*, Kephart states that for an individual kit, a pot no more than one quart is necessary and that it should fit easily into a knapsack. Swedish cook sets are great to fill this part of your kit, but unfortunately they are difficult to locate. Generally, they are made of both aluminum and stainless steel and come with a stove stand and Trangia stove; the lid becomes a shallow pan or drinking cup, and the main body is a 1.6-quart cook pot or "Billy Can." There are many similar cook sets available from European countries via surplus. A single 1-quart pot should not be hard to find. Zebra makes several sizes in stainless steel, and Self Reliance Outfitters offers bush pots in anodized aluminum as well as in stainless steel at the 1.8-quart size.

If you're not concerned about a lid for your bush pot, you can make one out of any stainless milking-style bucket or another metal container that is food safe. Drill bail holes near the rim of the container, using #9 trapping wire for a bail. The pot will become a familiar friend around the fire at night, and you will find after some time that anything cooked in your old friend tastes better. The bush pot provides a good dry storage space in the pack if it has a secure lid, and it can be a great place to keep fire-starting implements. A cook pot of some sort and a stainless steel bottle and cup gives you a pretty reliable combination for any condition.

POT HANGING

There are several ways to hang a bush pot over the fire for cooking or water heating. The most useful are the tripod, the crane, and the adjustable pot hook.

TRIPODS

Tripods are made by shear lashing three sticks of equal length, about 1½"–2" in diameter. These sticks should be wedged or pointed on the non-lashed end to help keep them from slipping on wet ground or snow. Leave enough length on the cordage so that after lashing, you can lash a toggle to the line, which you can adjust by wrapping over the tripod ends to vary the pot height over the fire. The toggle should be longer than the top span of the bail so as to hold by wedging. Lash the toggle using a V notch and a clove hitch knot. You can easily adjust the height by small amounts and move the legs of the tripod from side to side to control the distance of the pot from the flames. Don't fuss with the cordage or pot while you're moving the tripod.

CRANES

There are many types of **cranes**; some are fairly simple, others are more complicated affairs. Simple is always best, and most of the time it's more robust. The most basic crane involves a stick and fork. The long stick is sharpened on one end and notched with a log cabin notch on the other. Drive the point of the long stick into the soil, then place a stick with a Y fork underneath to hold the stick in place. These pieces can be adjusted to increase or decrease the angle raising or lowering the pot. The pot is suspended by the bail from the log cabin notch, which keeps it from slipping down the stick.

Simple pot crane

POT HANGERS/BAIL STICKS

Another method of suspending pots is by using a pot hanger, or **bail stick**. This stick should have multiple adjustment points to either raise or lower the pot on either a cross stick, two forks driven into the ground a few feet apart with a horizontal stick across the middle, or a crane with a flat angle on the top and divot to mate with the bail notches. If you use a cross stick, then you'll need several forks within the stick for adjustment. In the end, it is generally easier to carve notches for this task than find sticks in which such forks or notches naturally occur. Also, remember:

When using forks for making anything, don't use an actual forked branch, as these are prone to split. Rather, use a cutoff where another branch is growing from the tree so that you are pounding on a straight downward plane, and always split out the area to be struck with an axe to prevent it from mushrooming out.

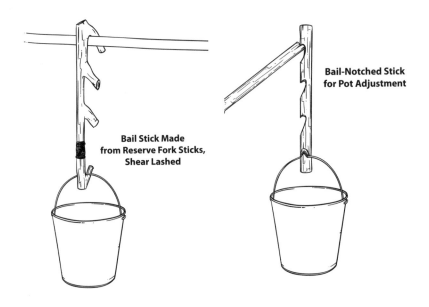

**Bail-Notched Stick
for Pot Adjustment**

**Bail Stick Made
from Reserve Fork Sticks,
Shear Lashed**

Pot hangers

SKILLETS

A skillet, a shallow cooking pan, gives the traveler the ability to fry foods as well as providing a plate from which to eat. Of course, we would not need the pan at all if we were satisfied to eat soups from the pot, ash cakes from the fire, or roasted meat from a green stick over the fire. But do you really want to do that? The pan gives us the ability, when used with some animal fats or grease, to fry our foods. For the longer journey, something fried can be a nice change for the palate.

The Swedish cook sets mentioned earlier have a lid that becomes either a shallow bowl or a skillet. However, if you don't own one of those sets, there are many skillets on the market made of aluminum, coated aluminum, stainless steel, and steel. It pays well to carry an extra pan because of its versatility. Try to get one that has a folding handle of some sort, or one with a socket into which you can insert a stick. If you're just looking for a plate either to store food while something else cooks or to eat from, many pot lids can be used for these purposes as well.

MEAT ROTISSERIE

You can fashion a simple meat rotisserie by using another forked stick as the horizontal between the two forks. Cut a point in the stick on the opposite end from the fork and then split it up to about 2" from the pointed end. Push the ends of the split stick through a piece of meat, then lash the splits together to squeeze pressure on the meat. Rest the rotisserie on two vertically forked sticks you've stuck in the ground on either side of the fire so the meat can be rotated when desired for even cooking. If the meat is a game animal, slide skewers through the meat and the forked stick to stabilize and hold the rib cage open; this will result in more even cooking.

BUSHCRAFT TIP

You can make almost all the cooking tools you'll need from natural materials, other than a bucket for disinfecting water and boiling meat. All of the cranes, pot hangers, and tools for food handling discussed in this section are made of sticks.

PLANKS

Planks are slabs of wood crosscut from a larger piece and used as a cooking surface for foods such as breads and bannocks. These planks should be of a non-resinous wood so as to not affect taste; hardwoods are also preferred so that the food can be moved close to the fire without risk of burning the wood while the pastry is cooking. You can use planks for cooking almost any breads or bread-related food, but the batter must be a bit thicker, as the plank is generally angled on another piece of wood or stone to expose the pastry to the heat. It is then rotated and maneuvered to take advantage of the best slow cooking heat from the coals and fire.

TOOLS FOR FOOD HANDLING

You won't need more utensils than the sheath knife and jackknife, as you can fashion any other utensil with these tools. One of the handiest items you will want is a scooping device for getting cooked food from the pot to your mouth. Many foods and liquids can simply be consumed by drinking them straight from the container, but if you want a spoon, it will not take much effort to carve one. Take a split branch about 8" long and 4" around. The split can be carved into a handle on one end, and either burned with coals from the fire to create the bowl or dished out with a knife. You can make a spatula in the same fashion; follow the same procedure as the spoon, but instead of hollowing out the bowl, cut the end flat. If you find that you need a fork, a simple forked stick will do the job, as well as any metal fork. (This might be necessary if you do not wish to eat your meat from the stick cooking it over the fire, or if you need to get a meat chunk from a pot.) If you need tongs, creating them is a simple project. Use a green branch, and cut in the middle of the branch. Then, bend the green branch in half. A simple stick will work for stirring sugar into tea or coffee.

When it comes to the actual cooking, flat rocks free of moisture can make a great grill top. Depending on the thickness of the stone slab, you can cook anything from eggs to steak on stone. Using stone as a fire backing will also hold good heat for cooking with other methods, such as a rotisserie. Stones arranged around a fire can be used for anything from pot or skillet warmers to actual baking.

CAST IRON

Cast-iron cooking has been the standard for good campfire cooking since the days of the pioneers. They say that nothing cooks like cast iron, and a good seasoned cast-iron skillet or pot is a family heirloom. The main issue with cast iron, however, is the weight. Unless you have some sort of conveyance (such as a canoe, a horse, or an ATV), you will weigh yourself down dramatically with even the smallest piece of cast-iron cookware. However, if you have the choice, cast iron provides ease and versatility in cooking around the camp or cabin. A 2-quart Dutch oven and a skillet in which the oven lid will fit is about as good as it gets for camp cooking.

BUSHCRAFT TIP

If you want your cast-iron pots and pans to stay seasoned, avoid washing them with soap. (Seasoned means the pores of the iron are saturated and filled with oil and grease; this makes the cookware nonstick as well as adding to the flavor of the food cooked in it.) When you're finished cooking with a nicely seasoned piece of cast iron, wipe it clean with a rag and put it away. If something gets stuck to the surface or you accidently burn food to the metal, fill it with water only and boil it over the fire, then wipe it and dry thoroughly. Never use a scrubbing pad or soap on cast iron. Most new cast-iron pans come pre-seasoned. If yours is not, or if you buy used and it is rusted, clean the rust with a piece of steel wool, wipe down with a heavy amount of cooking oil or lard, then heat over a fire. Repeat this process as needed until the oil stands in the pan. At this point, you can pour out the excess oil and wipe it down as usual.

COOKING IRONS

There are many types of cooking irons and implements made from ironwork by blacksmithing; the types covered in this section are the most useful and versatile for camp use. Iron is heavy, so if you're going to carry these, most of the time you'll need a conveyance of some sort.

"Squirrel cookers," as they are called, are a very useful type of cooking iron, made up of two pieces about the length of a bedroll. They can be used for cooking chunks of meat, for hanging a pot over the fire, or as a poker to stir the coals and arrange wood in the fire. Another use for these two irons is as a skillet grate if placed over a keyhole fire pit. To use the squirrel cooker as a pot hanger or meat fork, place the pot hanger end of the iron through the pig tail of the other iron, (that is, the part of the iron curled like a pig's tail) and then place the other end of the pig tail piece in the ground as an upright. This then becomes a crane that can be rotated for use as a pot hanger or meat fork, depending on which side is over the fire.

Another type of iron that is useful in camp is very similar to a wooden rotisserie. It features two uprights and a cross bar placed horizontally through the eyes of the two uprights. From this, a combination of hooks and chain or trammels are used to adjust pots over the fire or cook meat on the cross bar. These setups are a bit impractical for normal use, as they are heavy. They are very useful, however, if you can find a way to easily transport them.

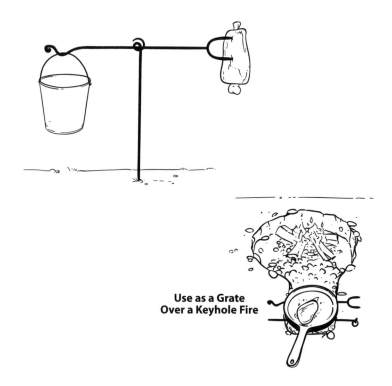

**Use as a Grate
Over a Keyhole Fire**

Squirrel cooker

STOVES AND BURNERS

The terms "stove" and "burner" really refer to two different things. "**Burner**" refers to the unit that produces the fire. A stove is the stand, grated material, or component on which the pot or cup rests *over* the burner. (The Trangia and alcohol "stoves" currently on the market are actually burners.) To avoid confusion, I will refer to burners in the following text as stoves, and stoves as "stove stands"—that way, when searching today's market, you will not be confused.

STOVES (BURNERS)

All alcohol stoves on the market, whether they are penny stoves, Coke can stoves, or traditional Trangia stoves, work on the same principle: an enclosed material wick (usually asbestos) is sealed in a confined space with holes at the bottom of the container for alcohol to wick in. There is a reservoir in the center into which liquid is poured so that it seeps into the wicking holes. After the alcohol is lit in the reservoir, which can be accomplished with a ferrocerium rod or open flame, the fumes rise from the wick within the enclosed vapor chamber and burn through tiny holes in the upper rim of the device, causing it to jet. Some people use different accelerants other than straight denatured alcohol in the devices, but I do not recommend this practice, since they will either clog the outlet holes or smoke heavily.

Most of the Trangia stoves that are the original design used in the Swedish cook set will burn about thirty minutes on one fill of alcohol, and boil one quart of water in about five minutes with a good stove stand. New model Trangia stoves on the market are passable as well, but the originals are the most robust. Many of them are available on the web for between $20 and $100 and will last a lifetime. The one component of the Trangia you may need to replace is the "O" ring used to seal the lid, allowing the stove to be stored in your pack when filled or partially filled with alcohol. The "O" rings can be purchased online, but you can also find comparable ones at most hardware stores. These stoves have stood the test of time and are far less susceptible to problems than are modern multi-fuel backpacking stoves.

STOVE STANDS

Stove stands are used to raise the pot or cup being heated above the flames of the stove (burner) to provide space between the burning jets and the bottom of the object, allowing oxygen flow. There are many small folding versions of these stands available;

however, many do not provide a windscreen. The stove stand that comes with the Swedish cook set was designed as not only a stove stand but also a windscreen that nests with the set, eliminating the need to carry two separate pieces of gear. The older stove stands made for the U.S. military canteen and cup are an open sleeve design that nested on the cup, featuring air holes to provide oxygen. Robert Simpson of CanteenShop.com recently designed a stove stand for the U.S. canteen cup that also provides a grill top to the stand and screen. Working with Self Reliance Outfitters, the folks at CanteenShop have also made stove stands for cups, canteen cups, and bush pots in stainless steel, which provide all of the benefits mentioned here. Keep in mind that any stand you use needs to nest within the cook set well, so it does not take up extra space in the pack. You can make a quick stove stand from any large soup can by cutting off the top and bottom of the can and then drilling several holes around the top and bottom third of the can to allow oxygen flow.

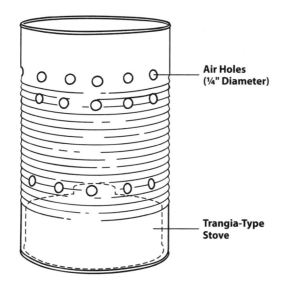

Air Holes (¼" Diameter)

Trangia-Type Stove

Simple stove stand made from a large soup can

TIPS AND TRICKS FOR COOKING IN THE FIELD

1. When you're cooking any type of meat, boiling will save the most nutritional value from the animal. Drink the broth as well; it contains critical fats.

2. Any stones used for cooking or placed directly within a fire should never come from creek beds or rivers. Even if they appear dry, they can still hold moisture that will cause a fracture when heated; they can create great danger from flying debris when they explode.

3. Fires are for warmth and coal beds are for cooking. Always let fires burn down to develop a large coal bed for cooking needs.

4. Always pick fire locations carefully, bearing in mind the wind direction and strength so that the flames do not get out of hand.

5. When you're leaving an area, fires should be completely out with no smoke coming from the coals. Crush carbon completely and scatter it to make the smallest impact on the land.

─ Chapter 5 ─
COVERAGE

"A pleasant stopping-place is seldom far to seek in a hilly country that is well wooded . . . In a level region, whether it be open plain or timbered bottom land, good water and a high and dry site may be hard to find."
—HORACE KEPHART, *CAMPING AND WOODCRAFT*, 1919

Choosing proper coverage for your expeditions will depend on your environment, the season, and the duration of your stay in the wild. A well-constructed shelter made of durable material can make the difference between a safe, warm, and dry night's sleep and a potentially life-threatening situation. To help you choose the best options for your kit, this chapter details many coverage options, from types of tarps to sleeping bags and blankets, and even natural shelters you can construct on the fly or in emergencies. You'll also learn essential skills for treating your coverage materials and creating tents, as well as folding and storing options for carrying shelters with your kit. From modern military Modular Sleep Systems with bivvy bags to traditional wool blankets and fire lays, here you'll find the information you need to choose and maintain essential cover elements—another one of the Five Cs necessary to create a microclimate of protection from the elements.

TARPS AND TARP TENTS

The biggest advantage of the tarp or tarp tent is that it provides a no-floor footprint. A waterproof floor in a tent can cause several problems:

1. Water can run under the tent and leak through; then the waterproof floor will form a holding bucket for this water.
2. If water infiltrates the tent from the top, the water will be contained by the floor.
3. With no airflow from under the tent or no place for moisture to escape, floored tents can become a nightmare of trapped condensation throughout the night.

Tarps and tarp tents are easy to carry and pack. They are also the most versatile for different setups, depending on conditions and seasonality. The most common materials for these items are polypropylene, silnylon (silicone impregnated nylon), canvas, or oilcloth. All of these materials have certain advantages, as well as disadvantages.

POLYPROPYLENE AND SILNYLON

Polypropylene is a lightweight material that can be purchased very inexpensively; however, its poor longevity and durability make it unsuitable for anything other than the short term. A seasoned camper would never want to own this for an often-used sheltering device because of its potential impact on the environment. Another problem with this material (which can be an issue with any material) is that tarps made from it always use grommets or metal rings for tie-out options, not actual loops sewn into the material and reinforced. It is always best to have established loops or actual tie outs instead of grommets, since the former offer better support and less stress on the material.

Silnylon, a nylon material impregnated with silicone for waterproofing, is by far the most popular material used today for shelter tarps and flies. The main advantage of silny is that it is very light and can be crushed into a very small package for ease of packing. The main disadvantage of this material for the bushcrafter wishing to spend a lot of time in the woods is that it is very susceptible to fire. A lot of companies are still using grommets in silny as well, which cause failure when the material is under stress. Many good silny tarps are available if you desire to use them, but keep in mind that, as with all other critical elements of your kit, you need them to be multifunctional and durable. You will never drag a deer out of the woods on a silny tarp without destroying the tarp.

CANVAS

Traditional **canvas** is one of the most resilient materials to use as a tarp or tarp tent. Today, many canvas tarps are more fire retardant and mildew resistant than in the past. This makes canvas a prime material for long-term use as a shelter (cover) component. The main disadvantage to canvas material is weight; anything over about 7' × 7' is too bulky for any use without some sort of conveyance. Many canvas tarps have well-sewn-in tie-out points, but you still need to avoid grommets.

Tarp tents of 8' × 8', 9' × 9', or 9' × 12' will be of the most use to the single traveler. I am very partial to Tentsmiths.com's Egyptian oilcloth for lightweight carrying and durability. If you are using this tarp for a season, it is important that it be resilient under varied weather conditions.

MAKING A CANVAS TENT

You can make a simple tarp tent from any painter's-type canvas drop cloth. A size of 9' × 12' will give a good number of options for setup, and it can be treated easily with products such as Kiwi Camp Dry or Thompson's Water Seal for quickness. You will need tie-out points on this canvas for driving stakes and running guy lines. Lay the tarp out on the ground; for each corner, take a marble, stone, or wad of leaves and bunch the fabric around this object, tying it off and leaving tails to form a loop. You will want one of these in each corner to start. After this is accomplished, fold the tarp lengthwise, and again make loops, not only at the corners but at the center as well, evenly spaced between the corner and center. Then, fold the tarp the opposite length, doing the same step as before, including the marble, stone, or bunch of leaves, adding a loop at each corner and at each side of the center, evenly spaced. Once this is complete, fold the tarp at its widest point halfway to center from both ends, and again make tie outs on the corners. You should now have seventeen tie outs for making several different setups easily. Tarp tent setups will be explained further in Part 2.

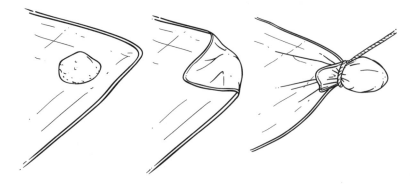

Tarp loop attachments with rocks

OILCLOTH

Oilcloth tarps are well suited for longer-term use, and because quality ones are made from high-thread-count cotton, they are fairly lightweight. An oilcloth tarp of 8' × 8' is easily manageable for packing and carrying. The only real disadvantage to oilcloth is that it will burn if exposed to direct flame. Some oilcloths are heavier than others, depending on the type of cotton used in its manufacture, but good Egyptian cotton is light and durable. Make sure that you have tie-out loops and not grommets.

MAKING OILCLOTH
You'll need:

❑ Painter's drop cloth of fabric weight more than 8 ounces
❑ 1 quart of mineral spirits, available as paint thinner at most home improvement stores
❑ 1 quart of boiled linseed oil, available at home improvement stores
❑ Concrete pigment (optional)

1. Machine wash and dry the drop cloth; this will close the fibers.
2. Mix the mineral spirits and linseed oil in 50/50 proportions. You will need this combination of chemicals. The linseed oil waterproofs the fabric, and the mineral spirits allow the oil to dry. If you use straight linseed oil, the fabric will not dry and will remain oily and sticky.
3. Shake the mixture well.
4. Add any type of concrete pigment to the mixture for the color desired.
5. Hang your tarp from a fence or line, and then brush-paint the mixture into the tarp, covering all areas evenly. Make sure it is saturated well.

6. Leave the tarp hanging until it dries, which should take about forty-eight hours. The smell will take about a week to disperse from the oilcloth. WARNING: Linseed oil is flammable, so be careful not to expose this tarp to direct flame.

GROUND PADS

There are many commercial **ground pads** on the market made from a variety of materials. Blow-up mattresses are prone to punctures, although they will fold up smaller than a foam pad. However, a foam pad is very resistant to tearing from sticks and roots, and is easy to dry when the ground is moist. I prefer an exercise mat from a local box store; the mat is black, so it absorbs heat. These are more flexible than traditional sleep mats, so they can be used for first aid purposes as well, such as stabilization of a dislocated knee or broken bone. Make sure that whatever you use will suit your purpose. Any ground pad must be thick enough when compressed to battle the effects of conduction (equalization of ground temperature to the body, causing heat loss), and yet be manageable for carry outside the pack.

BROWSE BAGS

A **browse bag** is made from lightweight material, which is sewn across one end and up one side, creating a body-length bag that can be used for a mattress when filled with browse (leaves or debris). Because the bag is made from a lightweight material, it can fold up small and take up little room, or add little weight to the pack. Browse bags can also be used as emergency sleeping bags and as an additional way to stay warm. The best thing about these bags is that they prevent conduction of cold temperatures from the ground; unlike ground pads, they take up little room in the pack. Be aware that it will take some prep time to set up your browse bag for proper use.

EMERGENCY THERMAL BLANKETS

Emergency thermal blankets are very useful within any kit. They can act as a heat reflector, blanket, ground pad, or tarp. Most of the reusable blankets (which is the type you should carry) are 5' × 7'. Most emergency blankets have at least a grommet hole in each corner. While this is not the most desirable method of attachment to a solid object for tie out, it can come in handy for emergency use. These blankets are a great, light resource to create a moisture barrier on the ground in your shelter. Place the reflective surface up in the winter and down in the summer for maximum efficiency.

HAMMOCKS

Hammocks have been used for hundreds of years, although they are fairly new to the modern woods tramper. Hammocks give the advantage of getting you off the ground above the critters, and when combined with a good tarp, they require little attention to keep dry—even in a driving rain. They are also very lightweight and packable, are quick to set up, and provide a very comfortable sleep. Most modern hammocks are made from nylon-type parachute materials, but they can be made from rope as well as canvas.

SETTING UP YOUR HAMMOCK

Hammock setup is not a complicated affair, and that makes them preferable when you're traveling quickly or trying to not add more weight. Most modern hammocks are tied off between two trees, using either heavy rope or strapping material such as nylon webbing. Most come equipped with carabiner clips that you clip to the straps. How taut you make your hammock depends on your personal preference, but keep in mind that a hammock's straps will stretch when first laid in, no matter how tightly you tie them to begin with. Some folks prefer them fairly tight, as they feel this gives better support when sleeping, but others prefer some slack.

Flying a tarp above the hammock for a waterproof roof makes a fabulous, easy camp outfit, especially in mild temperatures. You can use hammocks in colder environments or seasons, but special care must be taken to avoid convection because of the risk of hypothermia. To accomplish this, hang a thick sleeping pad or under quilt below the hammock. This will trap air between the hammock and the quilt, but not allow convective breeze to touch the bottom of the hammock that is against the body. You can also use a sleeping bag or wool blanket in conjunction with the hammock in colder weather. Pitching your tarp lower will also trap more heat that's released from your body.

SLEEPING BAGS

You will always stay the warmest by trapping warm air and sealing it into a space around your body. To this end, if you can confine the heat that naturally escapes from your body, you can stay warmer for longer periods. **Sleeping bags** help you do just that.

Sleeping bags are now the norm of camping. These days there are many types of synthetic material available for insulation fill and creating loft, or trapped air space, in these bags. Down- or feather-filled bags are available as well, and these varieties are very warm. However, these bags have a major downside when it comes to condensation and moisture collection: Over a few short days in the field, they become saturated with moisture from your body. If you practice bushcraft in dry and less humid areas, a good canvas-shelled and down-filled bag will be a welcome bed on a cold night.

MILITARY MODULAR SLEEP SYSTEM (MSS)

We now have synthetics for insulation, and few alternatives beat a **military Modular Sleep System (MSS).** With a Gore-Tex bivvy (a waterproof outer shell), this is a very convenient short-term option for just about any foul weather, especially if resources are scarce or environmental impact is restricted. In choosing what you need, remember that synthetic bags require drying out on a regular basis—and this may not be feasible, depending on season and geographic location. (For a normal dry environment, a synthetic bag may very well be the best short-term choice for the hunter.)

The MSS consists of an outer Gore-Tex bivvy for waterproofing and two inner synthetic-filled bags, one for lower temperatures and one for midrange temperatures. You can combine these bags in very cold conditions. There are also available a lot of military bags on the market from countries other than the United States, and you can purchase these fairly inexpensively. I have found the Swedish sleeping bags to be very roomy and warm when temperatures are around freezing. Combined with a single twin wool blanket, they make a great combination for less than $50.

BIVVY BAGS

The **bivvy bag** is a waterproof bag that covers your head and sleeping bag. It gives another layer of protection against cold and damp. Many bivvys are actually tube tents in which you sleep; they provide an enclosed breathable space that will repel bugs as well as most weather. Some bivvy bags, such as those used in an MMS, are Gore-Tex breathable shells that attach directly to the sleeping bag. These are waterproof and add additional insulation to your sleep system.

CARRYING

For carrying purposes, treat sleeping bags as you would bed-rolls—roll them up and suspend them from your pack.

WOOL BLANKETS

A wool blanket is by far the best choice for the longer term and for its sheer versatility, but to sleep comfortably with it requires a leaf bed or browse bag, and you may need to have a sizable fire in close proximity to the bed.

> **BUSHCRAFT TIP**
>
> For the wool blanket sleeper, understanding the rule of inverse squares relating to fire and use of log backings are absolutely critical. The rule of inverse squares means that the amount of heat felt from a fire at a given distance is reduced by the square root of that distance when one moves that distance farther away. Think of someone standing three feet from a fire. If the person moves only three feet farther away, he or she will only feel 25 percent of the heat felt at the original distance. Keep that in mind when deciding how close to or far away from the fire you want to set your sleeping blanket.

Many people argue that modern wool-mix blankets will keep you warm and dry while in the woods. This is correct, but you should know that the more wool in the mix, the more effective the blanket. Blankets made of 100 percent wool are water-resistant, flame-retardant, and warm, and retain about 70–80 percent of their insulate value, even when wet. A 70 percent wool blanket will be about 70 percent as effective as one that's 100 percent wool.

Not all wool blankets—even 100 percent wool—are created equal, and you must consider a few things before making your selection. Loom-woven blankets made by hand from virgin wools (that is, wool spun for the first time) will always be superior to machine-made blankets. A looser weave is somewhat desirable in this case, as it creates more loft when overlapped.

Carry one queen-size and one twin-size blanket, as this will offer the most options not only for sleeping but also for outerwear. This versatility gives the wool blanket a great advantage over other sleep arrangements, such as sleeping bags. If you cannot find thick wool blankets, use thinner blankets sewn together. Good Hudson's Bay Company–brand blankets can still be found at thrift stores, flea markets, and on places such as eBay at reasonably low prices.

NATURAL SHELTERS

The skill and knowledge to build natural shelters is the most important thing any beginning bushcrafter can possess. Why? Because adequate shelter is the most critical component for survival in the woods. You can carry many things easily on your person—even without a pack—the loss of which would be at least a serious inconvenience. Cutting tools, combustion devices, and containers can easily be attached to your belt, and cordage can be salvaged or carried in your pockets as well, but adequate shelter is another story. If for any reason you lose your shelter or it becomes damaged, you must know how to construct one using the materials you have.

There are many forms of natural shelters you can construct if you are without a decent tarp or tent. However, understanding what type of shelter to build and what materials to use is the key to controlling conduction, convection, and radiation. When building any natural shelter, the first consideration is the structural material that is available and workable in the area. Deadfall materials have the least impact on the environment, take the least physical effort, and are the least time-consuming to gather; however, you must ensure that they are structurally safe. Though they are dead, they may need to support considerable weight by the time you are finished. Any main supports (which should be at least 3" in diameter) should be cut green, if at all possible. External framework not supporting total weight can be constructed from dead fallen material with little risk.

There are three main forms of natural shelters: the **lean-to shelter**, the **A-frame shelter**, and the **debris hut**. However, you can construct any natural shelter to mimic a tarp configuration as well.

LEAN-TO

If the weather is fair and you can take advantage of the breeze, a lean-to-style shelter is best. You can make a lean-to by lashing a simple cross pole between trees. Add several more saplings at a 45° angle to the ground on one side, then weave in horizontal vines or cuttings. Once this is accomplished, waterproof the lean-to by adding more cuttings from bottom to top, layering them always with the growth upside down. (This will allow water to be channeled away from the shelter. If any cuttings are placed as they grow, water will collect toward the joints and run down into the shelter.) Avoid branches that can catch water or rain and drip inside the shelter.

Lean-to shelter

A-FRAME

For more inclement or stormy weather, add another side opposite to the first onto the lean-to shelter, creating an A-frame to
deflect rain or wind from two sides. Again, leave no branches or
supports from the inside sticking out, or the shelter will collect
water. The colder the weather, the thicker the thatching must be,
and if you want it to have insulative value, it must be at least 3'
thick with leaves and debris.

A-frame shelter

DEBRIS HUT

For the coldest of nights, especially if fire is not an option, a
debris hut will be a necessity. This is a simple modification of the
A-frame, with one end of the ridgepole on the ground, creating
a closed triangle structure with a small opening. The key to these
types of shelters is to remember that they only need to be large
enough for you—and nothing more. You must restrict space in
order to maintain heat on the inside, as it will all come from your

body and be trapped within. A bedding of leaves and debris on the ground of any shelter should be at least 4" thick when compressed to avoid the effects of conduction. Once inside, you can use your pack to close the hole through which you entered, like a trap door.

Debris hut shelter

TIPS AND TRICKS FOR SMARTER COVERAGE

1. When using your tarp for sheltering on the ground in colder weather, use debris or snow to help insulate around the edges. This will reduce any convective breeze from entering in those areas.

2. Hammocks make great chairs during the day when you set them up on a tripod lengthwise, with an open crossbar on the tripod.

3. If your tarp requires reproofing for water-repelling properties, a simple solution is to rub the entire tarp with a bar made from two parts beeswax and one part tallow or lard.

4. When using a browse bag as a mattress, if all available debris is wet, you can line the bag with a 55-gallon trash bag before stuffing to keep moisture from seeping through.

5. Never sleep closer than one full step away from any fire to avoid bouncing embers.

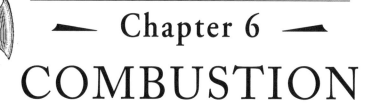

— Chapter 6 —
COMBUSTION

"Possessing the means and the knowledge to light fire at any moment is a prerequisite for living and surviving in the bush."

—MORS KOCHANSKI, 1987

From the beginning of time, man has needed fire, not only to warm his body but to cook and preserve his food, to light the dark walls of his cave when recording his hunts, and to give him something to watch as he fell asleep at night. Fire has been used to ward off animals that might otherwise prey on unsuspecting humans while asleep, and to keep away bumps in the night (imagined or real). Today, our needs for fire are no less important: We need the heat from fire for warmth on a cold night, we use fire to cook and heat water, and we use it to make our drinking water safe for consumption.

Since you know you need fire, you will need a combustion device as an element of your kit. There are numerous primitive ways to start a fire—so many that I could write a second volume to cover them—but remember, you are "smoothing it." You can practice your skills and "craft," but you need to be prepared as well. Fire is very difficult to create from only natural materials, especially in some environments, and it requires a high level of skill. There are three reliable methods of ignition readily available today:

1. The lighter
2. The ferrocerium rod
3. The magnifying glass (or "sun glass")

LIGHTERS

As with any other piece of gear, there are thousands of varieties of lighters available to you. Which is the best? It's the one that is the most reliable in foul weather, is the longest lasting over time in your pack when not in use, and has the ease of use when needed. The regular BIC brand lighter is the forerunner in this category. Lighters that require adding fluid fuels are prone to evaporation, and if they need parts replaced and are not a throw-away item, they are too complicated to be reliable. For ease of use, it is hard to beat flicking the BIC! Don't settle for the cheap imitations; get a real BIC, and if possible, get it in orange so you can readily find it.

You should have at least three lighters: one for the pocket, one for the belt pouch or haversack, and one for the main pack. The weight is negligible and the reward is great. The rule of thumb for a lighter or other open-flame device is five seconds to ignite tinder; any further use is wasting a resource.

BIC lighters have one significant problem: They are suscep-tible to cold. If the lighter itself is below 32°F, it will not light. Keeping one close to the body in a pocket is the best way to avoid this issue. If for some reason the lighter gets wet, it will not light until it is dry again. This can be accomplished by letting it sit and dry out or by removing the front housing and drying the actual striking wheel. Replace the dry wheel to make it function again.

FERROCERIUM RODS

Ferrocerium rods, metal match, misch metal—these are all synonymous terms. A ferrocerium rod is a solid rod made from pyrophoric materials such as iron, magnesium, cerium, lanthanum, neodymium, and praseodymium. Some of these materials have a very low combustion temperature, and when you create friction against the rod, combustion occurs. To accomplish this, you need a 90° sharp edge that is harder than the material of the rod. This harder edge will remove the material and create the spark that is approximately 3,000°F. For use in the woods, it is best to have the largest and longest rod possible, as this will increase the surface area and friction over distance. A longer rod will have more material removed when you strike it, and it will create more burning metal (sparks). I prefer to carry a blank rod that is ½" in diameter and 6" long, with the end wrapped in 1" duct tape. (This creates a handle and acts as an emergency flame extender as well.) Many rods have handles of plastic, wood, or even antler, but unless they are actually drilled and pinned, there is no epoxy that will keep the rod from eventually coming out of the handle. That being the case, you would do just as well to buy a blank rod and wrap it with tape that will not come off (unless intentionally removed).

Ferrocerium rods have very few problems. However, if you don't use the rod for some time, it may oxidize. You can remove this with the back of your knife, or you can add a light coat of spray paint on the rod and scrape this off during the next use. If uneven pressure is applied through repeated attempts at striking, you may also develop ripples on the rod itself. You'll need to remove these to make the rod function properly, as they will act like speed bumps during striking. To remove these, you need to use excess pressure to remove the extra material and make a flat striking surface again. If you properly strike the rod, it should take no more than three attempts to ignite tinder. If this does not happen, there is an issue with the tinder and you'll have to figure out what it is. The rod is a resource that should be conserved.

MAGNIFICATION LENS (SUN GLASS)

From the point of view of resource management for your kit, the **magnifying glass** or "sun lens" is really the best fire-starting method. If the sun is shining, you need only natural materials to make an ember. If you have made charred material, this will be easily ignited in seconds by the sun. Any lens carried should be at least 5x magnifications; size is actually more critical than power of magnification. The larger the surface area to collect the sun's rays, the better it will work. You do not need to go overboard in this aspect, however; a simple lens that is 1½–2" in diameter will work fine. There are containers for tinder with built-in glasses, called Hudson Bay Tobacco Boxes, which were designed to carry tobacco and then ignite the pipe. These work well for holding charred material and other fire-starting implements in a nice self-contained kit. The large lens from a broken pair of old binoculars or a Fresnel lens from any drug store will also work well.

KNIFE/AXE BLADES

You can also use the blade of your knife as an old-style flint and steel set to effect ignition, if the blade is of high-carbon steel and a good Rockwell scale hardness. This method will require the use of a rock such as flint, chert, or quartz that has a hardness rating of 7 or above. The rock is used to strike or drive material from the back of your blade. With this method, you are removing iron particles from the blade spine. These particles are pyrophoric, as with the ferrocerium rod, although these sparks will only be about 800°F. Unless a tinder-type fungus is used, this method will require a charred material for ignition of the ember. You can then use this ember to combust a tinder bundle or bird's nest.

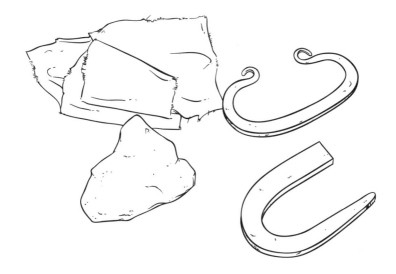

Flint and steel set

FRICTION FIRE (STICKS)

In this section, I will explain the basics of primitive ignition. There are many factors that can make a huge difference in ignition or failure, and most books make it sound much easier than it is. To start, understand that any fire requires heat, fuel, and oxygen to burn. You are aiming to create a coal; you will then transfer this coal to a nest and blow it into a flame. Creating a coal with this method requires a smoldering ember; this means limiting the flow of oxygen within the ember itself. The dust from the friction created between the two sticks is compacted into a small spot with little surface area to promote oxygen flow. Humidity and moisture of the materials are the biggest factors preventing ignition, so depending on the environment, these elements can greatly increase or decrease your success.

The other major factor for creating fire is your materials. You need materials that are fairly soft; they will be used as a board and spindle, so that downward pressure removes small particles of wood easily.

The preferred method for primitive fire-starting in the eastern woodlands is a **bow drill**. You need four pieces to make a bow drill. The handhold or bearing block is the piece that is the most difficult to manufacture in nature, since this portion of the set is where you want the least amount of friction to occur. This means that the handhold should be of a harder, denser wood than the spindle and hearth board. Any friction within the handhold will reduce the friction achieved on the hearth board, and make operating the set much more difficult and less energy efficient. The spindle portion becomes the "drill bit" that is meant to remove materials from the board to create the dust; the dust is ignited by heat caused by friction and speed. The spindle and the board should generally be made of the same materials. A good rule of thumb is that the material chosen should be made of wood in which your nail can make an impression.

Again, moisture content is the most critical in the two pieces of the set. The fire board or hearth is the bottom piece of the set that will be "drilled into," where the spindle will create the mound of minute shavings or dust to be ignited. Make the bow from any strong stick; if this stick has a gentle bend, that will help in the long run. It can be green or dead, as long as it is strong enough to hold a tight line or bow string, and is about 3' long.

Once your components are gathered, follow these general rules:

- The spindle should be approximately the diameter of your thumb, and the length from your thumb tip to your pinky finger tip with the hand outstretched, or about 9".
- The hearth board will need to be two-and-a-half times wider than the spindle, and about ½" in thickness.
- Form will be the other key element to your success with this method; you should always lock the wrist of the bearing block hand into your shin, and make sure the spindle is perpendicular to the board.

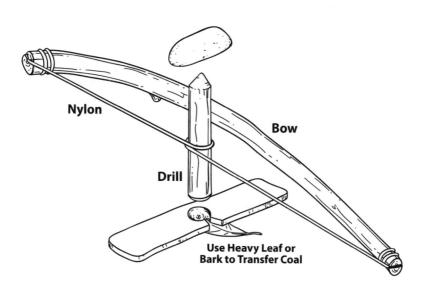

Nylon

Bow

Drill

Use Heavy Leaf or Bark to Transfer Coal

Bow drill fire kit

When starting to move your spindle on the board (to attempt to make a coal), do not rotate the spindle vigorously at first. Apply steady downward pressure, using the entire length of the bow string to achieve maximum revolutions for each stroke. As the dust begins to collect in your notch, you can then slightly increase your speed. This will cause friction heat that will ignite the collected dust into a smoldering coal. The biggest mistake most students make is going too fast right out of the gate. If you do this, you'll create heat but no material for ignition.

CHARRING TINS

Charring tins are an essential part of every woodsman's kit. A tin of some sort similar to ones used for Altoids mints or shoe polish works fine. You'll use this tin to create charred material to assist in the fire-making process, especially when bird's nests or conditions are damp. By quick ignition of charred materials, you will have a guaranteed ember to provide needed heat for ignition of a bird's nest. To use this tin, place some natural material such as cotton, punky woods, or the soft inner pith of plants inside. Close the lid and place the tin on the coal bed of your fire. By superheating the materials inside—but not allowing oxygen inside—you will create a carbonized charred material like charcoal. It is important to let the tin cool down before opening it, as the addition of oxygen to hot materials will cause combustion to occur. For a few swatches of cotton material about 2" × 2", it will take about ten minutes in a normal tin to create the char.

BUSHCRAFT TIP

To test your char, you can use any of the ignition sources you have. (This is the advantage of creating this material—a single spark should immediately create a glowing ember if done correctly.) Solar ignition with proper char should take less than 5 seconds of direct light with a sun glass. This is your safety net, in case you have not collected the proper materials for a bird's nest or tinder bundle along the trail or during the previous day, and must work with marginal materials.

TIPS AND TRICKS FOR SAFE, SUCCESSFUL FIRES

1. If you can find a tubular lamp wick, this can be used to cover your ferro rod to prevent oxidization when not in use. It also can be used to create an ember: Char one end by lighting it on fire, and then smother it out. This can be used with your ferro rod or sun glass to create an ember.

2. When it comes to fire, remember to practice the primitive methods, but always prepare by having your modern backups in case of emergency. Practicing with more primitive methods will give you a much better understanding of what it takes to manipulate the triangle of fire to get what you want.

3. A BIC lighter is a good gauge of ambient temperature. If you lay it outside on a blanket in camp and it will not light, the temperature is below freezing. If the temperature is above freezing, the BIC should light easily, provided it is in good working order to begin with.

4. Solar ignition is always easiest during the zenith hours of the sun, from 10 A.M. to 2 P.M., and will always be easier in summer than in winter.

PART 2
In the
Bush

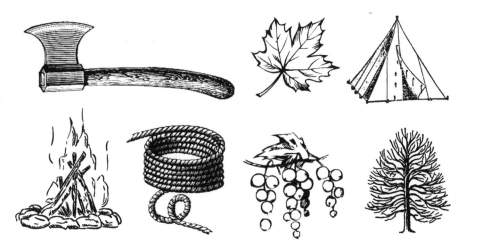

— Chapter 7 —

SETTING UP CAMP

"Shelter provides a micro-environment that supplements inadequate clothing or allows you to shed cumbersome layers, especially when you want to stop moving or when you want to sleep in cold weather. Shelter also enhances the effect of a warming fire."

—MORS KOCHANSKI, 1987

One of the most important decisions you can make while tramping is where you choose to establish your camp. Much of this decision is based on a simple set of rules (the Four Ws), but some other things to consider are:

- How long do you intend to stay?
- Are you only stopping for a quick lunch and a break?
- Are you staying only one night then moving on, or do you intend to make a base camp from which to work for several days?

Any camp you choose as a base camp for an extended period will need to be thought out more carefully, because of the eventual depletion of close resources.

THE FOUR WS

The Four Ws are a very easy yet important checklist of concerns to follow when choosing a proper camp location. They are:

1. Wood
2. Water
3. Wind
4. Widowmakers

WOOD AND WATER

The first W stands for **wood**. Be sure to ask yourself the following questions each time you stop to camp:

- Do I have a close source for the wood I need to accomplish any tasks I plan for this camp setting?
- Is there firewood to last the time I will be here?
- Is there enough deadfall, or will I need to cut wood? (Depending on what tools you have with you, this can be significant.)
- Are there construction materials close by that I can use to build shelter framing, cooking gear, or any other crafting I have planned?
- Is the wood that is available to me the proper species for either a warming fire or a cooking fire?

Generally, to build a quick-warming fire as well as for initial fire lays, you want softer species of wood, such as willow, poplar, pines, or cedars. If you are planning to cook and need a lasting coal bed without the resins and oils prevalent in some of these woods, you will want hardwood species such as ash, walnut, oak, and hickory.

The second W stands for **water**. As with wood, there are important questions to answer before you set up camp:

- Is there a water source within short distance of camp that will be convenient for easy collection?
- Is the water source a flowing source or standing source? A standing source will evaporate in summer and poses the threat of stagnation as well. Any ground-source water will need to be boiled at a minimum, but both filtering and boiling is preferred when possible.
- Is the water source large enough to hold food fish?
- Is the water attractive to other animals that will use it, such as frogs, crayfish, turtles, and the like? Is the source large enough to attract mammals to use it as a daily source of water?

These questions can help when you're making decisions about where to set up a base camp.

WIND AND WIDOWMAKERS

The third W is **wind**. Wherever you choose to camp, wind is a concern both for the threat of fires running out of control and for the ability to combat or take advantage of convective breezes. You also want to consider wind when pitching or flying a tarp, as the wind can blow smoke from your fire into your face or shelter through the night (which becomes a huge nuisance impeding your enjoyment of the camp). The elevation of your camp will affect the amount of wind to which you're exposed. Camping on a ridge will make you more susceptible to wind, but camping in low areas makes you more prone to cold temperatures. Remember that warm air rises and colder air sinks; for this reason, you should choose middle-high ground if feasible.

The fourth W stands for **widowmakers**. These are standing dead trees that may easily fall or break if subjected to wind. They could cause serious safety issues if they are close enough to fall into your camp area or the area into which you will frequently travel to get wood or water.

CAMP HYGIENE

Once you have chosen a camp location, you will need to think about hygiene needs in the form of waste disposal if you are camping for longer than one night. Urine as well as defecation should be kept far away from water sources. Both need to be kept away from camp so as not to invite bacteria and critters. Urine is a simple issue; you can just walk twenty steps or so in the opposite direction of camp and the water source and do the business straight on the ground or against a tree. Doing the other business, however, can require a bit more work if the stay will be longer term. If you are only there for a short period, you can simply dig a hole about 8–10" deep when the need arises and fill in the hole when finished, allowing everything to decompose naturally. If you are staying longer, a small, elongated trench may be in order. Dig this trench a bit deeper. With each visit, cover the deposit; with subsequent visits, you will move down the trench a bit at a time. Any group including more than one person camping for a few days will require a more elaborate system such as several trenches in different areas.

PERSONAL HYGIENE

For personal daily hygiene, I usually use the bandanna in my pack combined with ashes from the fire to create a quick solution that is antibacterial in nature when a bit of hot water is added. To make this solution, add white ash from hardwoods to water, in a ratio of three parts water to one part ash. I have washed my clothing in this same solution, and it will do a pretty good job when you're out of soap. This will do for washing, if needed, but simple fire smoke is antibacterial in nature for the very short term; standing over the fire and opening your clothing to let smoke in will kill many odors from perspiration.

Clean Teeth

I generally carry a toothbrush because, in my experience, it is far superior to any plant material or chewed stick for the job. (Plus, the thought of a splinter in the gums is enough to make the toothbrush more than worth the weight!) When brushing teeth in the short term, warm water will do a fine enough job; if grit is needed, mix ashes with water for this as well.

Clean and Dry Feet

One of the most neglected yet important matters that you must address daily is your feet. *If you cannot walk, you cannot tramp.* Many things affect your feet, and they need special attention so that you can maintain comfort while tramping. Boots for tramping should be well broken in, of course, and fit the needs of the environment in which you are operating. Summer boots should breathe well, and winter boots should be well insulated. Beyond this, pay attention to the socks on your feet, and always carry changes with you. Wet feet, no matter what the climate, are never comfortable for long. Socks should be changed often when hiking; expect to go through at least three pairs per day on longer treks. If you must sleep in socks, never sleep in the ones you wore all day; I do not recommend sleeping in socks in any case, unless you carry a special loose-fitting pair. Tight socks will restrict circulation and result in cold feet at night, even in a good bag. Feet should be well dried in the air or by the fire every night before turning in, and a bit of a smoke bath won't hurt either if you cannot wash them.

TARPS AND TARP SETUP

The cover element you use will dictate how you adapt to a given situation. This is the reason why I believe so strongly in tarps and tarp tents. Even if you are using a hammock, versatility is key to a comfortable night's sleep in any given scenario. It is important that you choose or make tarps that have the maximum amounts of points for tie outs, be it by loops or by actual tie-out tails. There should also be loops for pulling the tarp from the outside to increase the inside space.

The following instructions explain some of the most common tarp configurations. Before we begin, here's the basic vocabulary used for tarp and tarp tent pitches:

- When a tarp is set up without any of the fabric touching the ground, it is known as **flying the tarp**. This works very well for hammock-type setups.
- If any portion of the tarp's fabric is staked at ground level, you are **pitching the tarp**.
- To **pitch a camp** is to set it up, and to **strike a camp** is to take it down.

FLYING A TARP

Most often, when flying a tarp, you will use a ridgeline of some sort as a main support for the tarp. The tarp can be laid across this ridgeline either in square or diamond fashion when using a square tarp, which I highly recommend for the most versatility. The ridgelines I use are generally either a natural material rope of ½" diameter or a piece of 550 parachute cord 25' long. This length will give you plenty of room, in case the trees are farther apart than desired. Follow these instructions for a foolproof setup:

1. Tie a bowline knot at one end of your ridgeline rope or cord. Tie an overhand knot with a 2" tail, to be used as a stop knot, on the other end.

2. Pass the rope around a tree or main tie-out location, and then feed the tag end through the bowline. This will create a self-tightening loop that will not lock (for ease of adjustment) but will remain secure under load.

3. Once the other end of the rope has been passed around an opposing tree, create a trucker's hitch, leaving a loop that stops on the stop knot. This allows you to secure one corner of the tarp by passing this loop through a tie out on the tarp, and then placing a simple toggle in the rope loop, drawing it down to tighten the tarp. This will come out easily, if needed, for striking camp or making adjustments later.

4. The best thing to use on the opposite end of the tarp is a simple prusik knot made from a 6" loop of line. After tying the line to the ridge, pull the loop through the opposite tie-out loop and toggle it. You can then slip this along the line until the tarp is tight to the ridge and it will hold by friction, making adjustments and striking easy.

5. At this point, stretch the tarp to the desired height on the two or four corners, and either guy it out with lines to another object or stake the lines to the ground. It is important to be sure that these lines are easily adjusted as well, because many tarp materials will stretch, depending on weather. Adjustable lines make tightening easy.

THE LEAN-TO

You can build a simple lean-to with either a rectangular or square tarp by attaching two opposing corners to a ridgeline, as described earlier, and staking the other side of the tarp to the ground with stakes. The most important thing to understand here is that the pitch or angle of the tarp controls important factors, such as how much heat will be held in and whether rain easily enters from the front.

DIAMOND OR PLOW POINT SHELTER

One of my favorite and quickest tarp shelters to set up is the **diamond shelter**. Again, this is best made with a square tarp. Attach one corner of the tarp to a standing object such as a tree or to one end of the ridgeline only. Stake the remaining three corners to the ground, creating a diamond-shaped shelter. This type of shelter has many advantages, especially when used with the ridgeline, as it can be quickly adjusted to create a lean-to during fair weather. It is great for completing camp tasks under cover from the sun and gives three-sided cover at night or during inclement weather. If your tarp has outside loops, you can guy a centerline loop out to another object to create more room on the inside, or you can use a stick on the inside to accomplish this.

TARP TENTS

Tarp tents are usually square tarps with extensions to the front that become doors when a center pole is used or when the tarp is secured to a ridgeline by the center tie-out point. This creates a three-sided structure with two flaps used as doors to create a full enclosure. You can fashion a tarp tent from a large rectangle tarp as well, but you will have to carry a larger-than-normal tarp to get the same effect as a manufactured tarp tent. The biggest advantage to tarp tents is their versatility. They can be used for all configurations of a normal tarp, with the advantages of a tent if needed.

GROUND CLOTHS

A **ground cloth** of some kind will come in handy not only as a moisture barrier but also as a convenient place to set yourself or your gear off the direct ground. You can fashion it from any scrap material that is waterproof (if possible), but it does not need to be any larger than the length and width of your body so as to keep your kit light. A ground cloth large enough to be folded over can be incorporated into a bedroll configuration. In fair weather tramps, you can forgo a tarp altogether.

FIRECRAFT

Fire-making is the most important skill for any woodsman to master. With fire, you can warm yourself, dry your clothing, and make your water potable. These are the simplest of things you may need from your fire on a daily basis around camp, but its usefulness goes further than any individual piece of kit. You'll need fire to cook your food, to create needed ash, to char materials for future fires, and to keep away the boogieman in the middle of the night. By the fire, you will spin the yarns of your adventures and dream of future ones. The campfire is the television of the woods, ever changing and surfing the channels as it burns through the night.

THE TRIANGLES OF FIRE

All fires need three components to burn: **ignition** (or heat), **oxygen**, and **fuel**. By understanding and controlling these inputs, you can master fire. If you add to or limit any of these inputs, you will change the outcome. This means you can create a warming fire, create a cooking fire, or make charred material for creation of your next fire.

Fuel is further divided into a second triangle: **tinder, kindling**, and **fuel**. These are major inputs that will either increase or diminish your chances for success, especially when conditions are less than optimal for building a fire to begin with.

- *Tinder* is the most highly combustible material within the fire's components. It can be made up of many things from natural to man-made materials, but should readily take a spark or easily catch fire when a smoldering ember is added.

- *Kindling* is made of natural materials that are pencil size or smaller in diameter. You will want about two-thirds of your initial fire lay to be made up of this material.
- *Fuels* will be anything bigger than kindling, up to and including logs, depending on the nature and need of the fire you are using.

STARTING MATERIALS

In Chapter 6 we discussed the major components of your fire kit:

❑ Lighters
❑ Ferrocerium rods
❑ Magnifying glass (sun glass)
❑ Char tin

Together, these materials provide the means to start fire. Now you need your starting material: tinder.

BIRD'S NESTS

A **bird's nest**, as an element of the fire lay, is a bundle of highly combustible material shaped and formed to mimic the nest of a bird. What is imperative to understand is that it truly needs to be like a bird's nest: a combination of fine, medium, and coarse materials that are highly combustible, such as inner and outer barks from softwood trees such as cottonwoods and poplars. Grasses and weeds will work for this, as well as birch barks, but some barks have other properties that will be discussed later. A bird's nest is used in combination with an ember, either created from char or from another method such as a bow drill. It must be of a size that will sustain flame long enough to light kindling. A good rule of thumb for tinder is to make sure it is softball size or larger.

Bird's nest

IGNITING THE BIRD'S NEST

The bird's nest is best used when materials are slightly green or damp, and it may take the ember some extended time to effect ignition. When using this method, keep the nest separate from the actual fire lay and place the ember inside the bird's nest where the egg would be. Raise the nest just above your mouth level, remembering that heat rises. Blow lightly on the ember to heat the surrounding materials. As the ember and material glow brighter, you can increase airflow until the nest flames, then rotate it 180° to make the flames rise through the materials. Then, place this burning bundle into the fire lay itself.

TINDER BUNDLES, TWIG BUNDLES, FLASH TINDERS, AND PINE RESINS

Tinder bundles differ from a bird's nest in that they are placed at the base of the fire lay and generally ignited without the use of an ember. For this method to succeed, the tinder must be dry and combustible enough to readily take a spark from your ferrocerium rod. This bundle is similar in materials, size, and nature to the bird's nest, except that there is no need for prolonged heat from an ember. You can combine tinder bundles and bird's nests with a twig bundle to prolong the time needed to make a fire sustainable, which gives you more time to find materials to add to it.

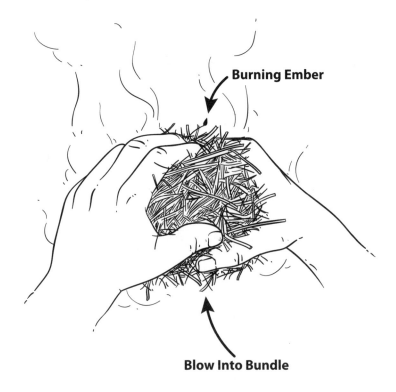

Burning Ember

Blow Into Bundle

Tinder bundle

Twig Bundles

A **twig bundle** can be used alone or combined with bird's nests or tinder bundles. The most effective way to ignite this tinder is to apply an open flame from a lighter. This will allow you to somewhat forgo the tinder leg of the triangle by applying excessive heat to combustible materials, such as dry weed stems and weed tops. Wrap a twig bundle under a nest or tinder bundle, and then turn the flame over onto itself. Allow the flame and heat to rise through the twig bundle; this is the most effective method, if used without open flame. Then insert this burning bundle into the fire lay.

Pine twig bundle with tinder

Flash Tinders

Some plant materials are what we call **"flash tinder."** They contain volatile oils that will readily combust, but because of the fine fibers involved, they will burn very quickly and the flame is short lasting. When these are combined into a bird's nest, they can be very effective. They can also be used in tinder bundles for the same purpose. The best examples of flash tinders are thistledowns and cattail fluff.

BUSHCRAFT TIP

Many trees have natural oils and **resins** that act as accelerants. These can be very useful, as barks and wood will have a much longer burn time than plant fibers. The two most significant sources for your purpose are birch barks and pine resins. Both of these require different types of processing. Birch bark can be peeled from the tree, but its intended use will decide the type of processing. Remember that any time you are attempting ignition by sparks from a rod, you will need lots of surface area to catch the sparks. The same holds true with barks such as birch; you'll need to shred it as finely as possible to expose many surfaces that can be ignited by sparks. If you have an open flame, the bark will readily burn straight off the tree.

Pine Resins

Pine resins can be used in a lot of ways; the dripping sap from a wounded pine is highly flammable, and you can simply spread it onto dry material and ignite it with a rod or flame. These resins will also settle in the tree itself, creating what is called **fatwood, pitch wood,** or **lighter pine.** Most pine trees have resin-soaked areas of the wood at any place there is a joint—for instance, where a branch comes out from the tree. On a dead pine, the resins will run to the bottom toward the roots. Standing dead pines are the best for this wood, but a fallen dead pine can hold good resources as well.

This wood will smell of turpentine and is very combustible with open flame. However, you can further process it to make it even more usable for a fire kit:

- Scrape this resin-laden wood with the spine of your knife, creating a pile of fine shavings. The shavings will combust quickly with the hot sparks from your ferrocerium rod.
- Create feather sticks.

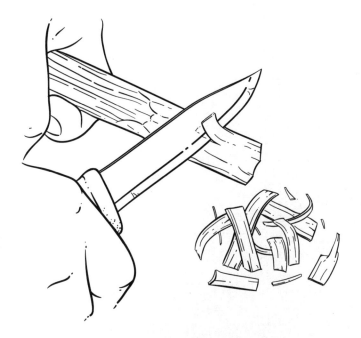

Cutting shavings from fatwood

FEATHER STICKS

Making feather sticks is a fantastic way to increase your kindling. If small dry sticks are not available, soft woods make the best feather sticks.

Shave a series of small curls of thin wood on a larger piece of stick. If this wood is fatwood pine, you'll have an accelerant to make this kindling even more powerful. By creating feather sticks, you're increasing surface area and allowing flames to heat the material faster, making it burn faster. A good feather stick will have several of these fine shavings on the same plane, and each will have several curls. Feather sticks can make up the entirety of a tinder pile used for a fire lay, if need be.

Feather stick

FIRE LAYS

The type of **fire lay** you set up is determined by your needs. Here we will discuss a few basic lays. Beyond the size of your tinder bundle and the amount of kindling needed to create a good sustainable fire, the two rules to remember are:

1. More oxygen is generally better. This does not mean that you should blow or fan your fire from the time you ignite it until it is sustainable; rather, it means that you must have a lot of space between the kindling so that oxygen can flow into the fire.
2. Fire loves chaos. This means that you do not need to stack things in neat piles to make a good fire lay. Picture the old childhood game of pick-up sticks—that is what chaos looks like in your kindling.

Another major rule to remember when starting a fire is that no fuel should be added to any fire until flames have risen above the current fuel level. This will keep you from depriving the fire lay of precious oxygen.

> **BUSHCRAFT TIP**
>
> Most people I see who fail at fire building during classes at my school do so because the fuel they are using is too big for the current heat coming from the fire. Remember that the smaller in diameter the fuel, the faster it will burn. Add kindling until you can see a visible bed of coals, and then begin to add fuel.

TEEPEE FIRES

The **teepee fire** lay is the one that I use the majority of the time to start my initial fire. It is very useful because of the updraft created, which allows oxygen to enter from the bottom and heat to rise to the top quickly. The best fires take advantage of the **Venturi effect** (updraft). Place many sticks in a stack fashioned like a teepee, their tips touching at the top, with a tinder bundle or bird's nest inside the teepee so that the heat rises into the sticks and the flames heat along the vertical length of the materials.

Teepee fire lay

LOG CABIN FIRES

The **log cabin fire** lay is best used in optimal conditions with very dry wood. It is reminiscent of playing with Lincoln Logs: You create a square box of fuel with a pile of kindling and tinder inside. Lay the larger pieces across one another; the space between them gives oxygen a chance to flow into the lay. The tinder and kindling are usually lit by open flame in this type of fire lay.

LONG FIRES

When shelter is not optimal and the weather is very cold, a **long fire** can be a lifesaver for a comfortable night's sleep. A long fire is just what it sounds like—a fire that's built in a long line, parallel to your body when you're asleep. To build a long fire, you will need some large deadwood or dry standing dead wood that you can cut down. Long fires should be as long as you are tall and placed approximately one full step from the area in which you intend to sleep. It is usually prudent to build a wall of logs behind the fire, which will absorb heat and become a thermal mass heater. These are often called reflectors, although without a reflective surface, they really only hold heat and push it by convection back toward your camp. These back walls should be as high as the top of your shelter, and the fire should be placed in such a way as to obtain a cross breeze to help feed it oxygen. For a long night in cold weather without proper shelter, maintaining a long fire will take enough wood to fill a regular-size pickup truck as high as the cab. Picturing this alone tells you the work involved and calories that will be spent just gathering this much wood. If such a fire is necessary, you should begin setting up at least four hours before sunset.

DAKOTA FIRE PITS

If you really want to take advantage of updraft to accomplish a hot burning fire, build a **Dakota fire pit**. These work very well if the materials to be burned are green or damp, or if you need excess heat for a project such as pit forging.

Dig two holes approximately 2' apart, about 14" in diameter, and 6–12" deep. These holes are then connected by digging a tunnel between the two. In one hole away from the downwind, build the fire lay. In the opposing upwind hole, dig an angle on the edge facing the wind. That will maximize airflow into the tunnel.

Air Flow

6"–14"
Opening

8"–10"

6"–8"

10"–12"
Opening

Dakota fire hole

This type of fire has advantages and disadvantages. It will burn very hot, so if you're burning substandard material, this method will utilize the material most effectively. However, fuel consumption will also be at a maximum, so if resources are short, this is not a good setup.

KEYHOLE FIRES

This type of fire is the best for cooking. To set up a **keyhole fire** pit, dig a small hole for your fire (how deep will depend on the size of the fire you want). At the front of this hole you will dig a trench at the same depth as the fire hole, so you can drag coals from the heart of the fire to create a cooking area over the trench. The resulting fire pit resembles the shape of a keyhole. This works particularly well if you are using a pan to cook with or if you are roasting your food.

TIPS AND TRICKS FOR YOUR CAMP

1. If your shelter location does not have good drainage because of the environment and you cannot get yourself off the ground, you can trench around your shelter to guide water runoff.

2. Old files are generally tempered very hard and will make passable fire steel for flint and steel ignition, if you grind off the edges. When doing this, be sure to take it slow and dip the file in cool water to preserve its temper.

3. After your fire has been kindled and you are working to make it sustainable, never add fuel until the flames are above the current level of fuel.

4. Always use green sticks and wood when building tools such as rotisseries for cooking. Never use resinous wood such as pine; instead, use hardwoods such as hickory or ash.

5. Coating ironwork such as firesteels with beeswax when hot will help preserve them and prevent rust.

— Chapter 8 —

NAVIGATING Terrain

"Knowing where you are is unnecessary. What you need to know is how to get back to where you were."

—DON PAUL, 1991

Navigation is an underrated skill for any woodsman. Even finding your way back to camp from a short scout should always be managed with some verification method in case you get turned around. Not only is it important to understand all aspects of map and compass, but you must also develop a sense of direction and travel by paying close attention to where you have been and where you are going. Learning terrain feature association and using hand rails will assist you greatly when traveling short distances, but for making long treks the map and compass are the keys to success.

COMPASSES

Not all compasses are created equal, and there are many types on the market today. I have always made sure that every piece of equipment I carry is both optimal for its intended use and multi-functional. The compass is no different. Your compass should act as a:

- Navigational device
- Signaling device for emergencies
- Mirror used for first aid as well as daily hygiene
- Tool capable of fire-starting by solar ignition

With these functions in mind, you can begin to picture the type of compass you should choose. You want a **baseplate compass** made for map reading. This compass has a flat plate, usually made from plastic, that can be laid on the map and is transparent for use in conjunction with mapping and factoring routes on a map with your compass. It also has a movable **bezel ring** that rotates on the compass, on which the degree readings are marked, preferably with glow-in-the-dark paint. This will make it easy to dial in a travel bearing both from the map and by using the visual bearing method discussed in this chapter. Make sure the compass has a mirror as well as a magnifying glass of 5x. When it comes to your compass, I recommend spending the money to buy a good one; that way, you will trust it when it's needed. If you want, you can carry a backup compass, but it will never replace a true baseplate compass made for map reading and navigation.

WHY CARRY A COMPASS?

The answer to this is not as obvious as it sounds. General direction-finding does not require a compass; in fact, on sunny days, you are your own shadow stick! In the Northern Hemisphere, if you are facing the sun you are looking in a southerly direction: southeast (SE) in the morning, southwest (SW) in the evening, and generally south (S) during the zenith hours from 10 A.M. to 2 P.M.

BUSHCRAFT TIP

If there is no sun, the trees will tell you the answer. All trees have one thing in common: They all have to effect photosynthesis to live, so the most branches will be on the side of the tree facing in a southern direction. Look at several trees to verify your conclusions.

The most important reason to carry a compass is *so that we can walk a straight line over distance.* Everyone experiences what is called **lateral drift,** which causes us to gradually move left or right over long distances when walking. If you can see an object, you can easily walk straight toward it. However, if you go down a hill or an obstruction blocks your view of your intended destination, you will no longer walk the same straight line. This is why you carry a compass.

BASIC COMPASS USE

Beyond determining direction, the basic use of a compass is to establish a **bearing.** If your compass has the movable bezel ring with degree readings, you will be able to perform this task. Most compasses have a needle that is two different colors, usually red/ white or orange/white. The white side of the needle points south, and the colored area points north. The "front" or "top" of the compass is where the mirror is, so if you open the compass and look into the mirror, your compass is pointed to the front. Under the bezel ring of the compass should be an outlined arrow or set of lines that move as the bezel ring is moved. This is important because you'll use this to "plug in" a visual bearing.

TAKING AND FOLLOWING A BEARING

Once you understand the component parts of the compass, taking a visual bearing and following it is easy. Use the sighting device on your compass lid (this usually looks like a "V" gun sight) to aim at a distant object. Hold the compass centered on your body with your arms stretched partway out in front of you, away from your body. Tilt the mirror enough that you can see both the object in the distance through the "V" and the bezel ring on your compass. The needle on your compass will always point north, so at this point move your bezel ring so that the outline, or "doghouse," lines up in such a way that the north needle is inside. You will then have the bearing at the top of your compass. At this point, if you lower your compass and keep the north needle within the line in the bezel ring as you walk, you will be walking a straight line or exact bearing.

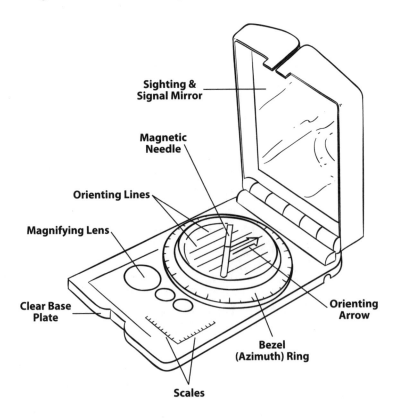

**Sighting &
Signal Mirror**

**Magnetic
Needle**

Orienting Lines

Magnifying Lens

**Clear Base
Plate**

**Orienting
Arrow**

**Bezel
(Azimuth) Ring**

Scales

Survival compass

LEAPFROG FOR LONG-DISTANCE TRAVEL

Trying to watch the compass as you walk may not be safe, in which case you'll need to leapfrog. To do this, you will use the bearing you just plugged in to sight on an object closer to you toward which you can walk without losing sight of it. Once you reach the object, pick another point on the same bearing and walk to it, and so on, until you get where you wanted to go. If you are given a bearing to follow or you have checked your map to get a bearing, you can place that degree reading at the top of the compass and rotate your body until the needle is in the "doghouse." At that point, you are facing the direction of the bearing, and you can proceed, either in a continuous movement or by leapfrogging.

UNDERSTANDING TERRAIN FEATURES AND MAPS

Remember that a topographic map is a two-dimensional image of a three-dimensional surface. So if you understand what you are looking at on the map, you can visualize what it looks like in real life. Here we'll discuss the five most prominent colors and five most useful terrain features on any topographic map.

THE FIVE COLORS

1. **Brown** is used for contour lines. These lines show elevation; generally, contour lines are in increments of 20'. If you can find an elevation level written on a line near a hilltop, this will help determine the contour level. For example, if a contour line is 800', then 5 lines above that will be 900', and 5 lines below will be 700'.
2. **Green** is used for vegetation. Generally, the darker the green, the more dense the vegetation.
3. **Blue** is used for water sources, creeks, streams, rivers, lakes, ponds, and so on.

4. **Black** is generally a man-made object of some sort, such as a trail, a railway, or a building.
5. **Red** shows major roadways such as highways.

THE FIVE TERRAIN FEATURES

1. **Hilltops** are the highest point of elevation in a rise, offering opportunities for overlook.
2. A **ridgeline** is a series of hilltops. These areas will enable high ground travel; animals use them for the same purpose.
3. A **saddle** is a low area between two hilltops. These areas offer good windbreak for camps without sacrificing elevation. Hilltops and ridges drain through saddles into valleys below.
4. A **draw** is the reduction in elevation from a saddle with high ground on both sides. This is usually a good runoff point for water and in many cases leads to a valley.
5. A **valley** is a low elevation running between ridgelines. These areas hold runoff and are the best places to look for unmarked streams. If they hold water, the higher ground above them will be excellent for ambushing game that goes to the water to drink. Most valleys are also good trapping locations.

READING OTHER MAP DETAILS

Once you can read the basic features of the map, you need to understand the other information that it can provide. The map can give you distance from one point to another, as well as show you the differences between what your compass is reading (called magnetic north) and the what the map has laid out (called grid north). This information will be important if you plan to travel using your map to obtain bearings.

The **map scale** is a reference usually at the bottom of the map that tells you how many inches on the map equal a certain distance on the ground. Maps are scaled in numbers like 1:10,000. This means that 1" on the map represents 10,000" on the ground.

The scale bar on the map makes this easier for you by showing a measuring device broken into inches or centimeters so that you can accurately measure with a ruler and convert that to distance. It is also important that you decide whether you are going to work with the U.S. system of measurement or the metric system when making calculations. Most of the examples I use in this book are in metric system, as I find everything divided by tens to be easy math.

ORIENTING THE MAP

For rudimentary navigation, you do not need to worry much about the declination differences between grid north and magnetic north. However, if you are trying to be very precise over distance and intend to take your bearings from the map, you will need to understand this process. Your map contains a **declination diagram**, which will show you the amount of degree offset left or right between magnetic north and map north. The top of any map is oriented north. Think of straight up on the map as corresponding to the hands of a clock pointing to 12. Magnetic north is actually left or right of 12 o'clock, depending on where you are standing on the earth's surface. Your compass always points to magnetic north, but the map is made to linear and lateral direction, so north on the map is not magnetic north. This difference is indicated in the declination diagram as a **degree of offset**. Once you find the declination diagram, you can do one of two things:

1. Set the declination difference in your compass if it has adjustable declination.
2. Use the calculation based on the degree of offset on every bearing you take from the map when planning your route.

Orienting the map is important if you want to match the two-dimensional image on the map to what you're seeing in the landscape before you. It is also important if you are planning a route while basing your planning on the map alone. To orient the map, place your compass fully opened on one corner so the straight edge of your compass and the grid lines on the map are parallel. If you are using this map to figure a route and to factor travel bearings, to start this operation you will need to either have the declination difference set on the compass or offset your bezel ring that amount from 360° at the top of the compass. When you've done this, rotate the map until the north needle is again in the doghouse. The map will be oriented to the terrain in front of you. Make sure that when you begin this procedure your map compass top is toward the top of the map.

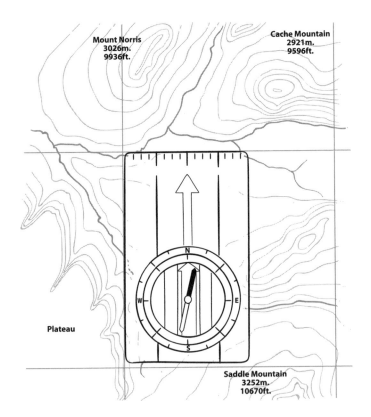

Orienting the compass

MEASURING DISTANCE AND TAKING BEARINGS

Once you have found the scale on the map, you can use any device for measuring, from a string with knots tied in it to a piece of paper with tick marks the same distances as the scale. Laying this object between Point A and Point B, you can calculate distance to be traveled.

TAKING A BEARING OR AZIMUTH FROM THE MAP

Once the map is properly oriented, you can use your compass to take bearings or **azimuths** from the map. ("Azimuth" and "bearing" are fairly synonymous words, meaning the direction of travel.) To do this, do not move the map. Lay your compass with the straight edge between the point where you are and the point you want to get to. Then rotate the bezel ring until the needle is in the doghouse. The bearing at the top of the compass will be your travel bearing.

FIVE NAVIGATION METHODS EVERY WOODSMAN SHOULD KNOW

1. **Handrails** are linear objects within the terrain you can use as a guideline to follow when they lead in the intended direction of travel. A creek bed, ridgeline, river, or roadbed could all serve this function to help you navigate to a location without following a compass bearing.

2. **Backstops** are a point you know you should not go beyond. These are generally linear land features that run perpendicular to your intended destination. A backstop could be a river, stream, roadbed, or railway. It need not be right on top of the intended destination, but it should be close enough that you'll know, if you hit that feature, that you have passed your mark.

3. **Baselines** are the opposite of backstops; these are used for returning to where you started from and should run

perpendicular to a campsite or base camp. When you've arrived at the baseline, you should understand which way to go to get back to camp without having to be precisely accurate with a compass bearing.

4. **Aiming off** is (usually) done in conjunction with a baseline. You will purposely take a bearing left or right of the intended destination a few degrees, so that you know on arrival to turn left or right to arrive at the desired location.

5. **Panic azimuths** are created so that if you get lost, you have a bearing to immediately plug into your compass that will take you to a known point. For instance, say you are traveling north, and off to the east is a river that is not a part of your intended travel route and is not a handrail. However, if you get lost, you know that a direct west azimuth from the river will take you back toward your intended course. From there, you can use that as a baseline to get your bearing for travel again or get you back on track.

REVERSE OR BACK AZIMUTHS

Sooner or later when traveling by compass, you will stray off course. When this happens, you should attempt a **reverse azimuth** to return to the last known point. A reverse azimuth just means traveling 180° in the opposite direction from where you were going. The easiest method is to simply look at your compass as if it were a clock. If your current bearing is at 12 o'clock, rotate the bezel to the 6 o'clock number, and you have the reverse azimuth.

DETERMINING DISTANCE WHEN TRAVELING

An important thing to realize is not only how far you have to travel but also how far you have traveled already. It is great to look at a map, break out a measuring device, and know your destination is

2.5 kilometers—klicks—east of you. But how do you know how far you have walked once you are on the way? **Pace beads** are the answer to this question; these are used to measure distance traveled.

To use them, create two strings of beads: one strand of nine beads and one strand of four beads. These are used to count 5 kilometers. Each bead on the side with nine beads represents 100 meters, and each bead on the side with four beads represents 1 kilometer. You will start with all beads at the top of the two strings, and drop beads accordingly as you travel in 100-meter increments. The key to this is figuring how many paces it takes to walk 100 meters.

To figure your **pace count,** or how many paces it takes for you to travel 100 meters over land, you must consider several factors. You should have a journal in which you keep personal notes for use in and around camp. Within this notebook you should record your pace counts. Check your pace in all terrains and always with the gear you intend to carry. Record your pace for flat terrain, uphill, downhill, uneven ground, etc. This way you can average, when needed, for multiple terrains. Your pace counts are figured in full paces, so if you step off with your left foot, your count will be on every strike of your right foot.

FINDING YOURSELF (SELF MAPPING)

Some folks assume that having a map and a compass will keep them found. However, if you don't keep track of where you are and wind up lost, it can be very difficult to figure out where on the map you are.

If you can find even one identifiable feature that is on the map, you may be able to complete **resection** to find where you are. Look from high ground at two different features on the map. Maybe you have found a fire tower and you can see two hilltops from where you stand. If this tower is the only one on the map, you're all set, but to verify this it would be good to do resection from the tower.

Take a bearing on the objects you can see from where you are standing and use the reverse azimuths to draw lines on the map. If these lines intersect at the fire tower (in this case) from the two hilltops, you have verified your suspicions that the tower is the one you can see on the map. This sounds easy in this example, but in deep woods or summer growth it can be nearly impossible, so it's best to watch the map from the start and navigate by all the methods listed here to stay aware of your current location.

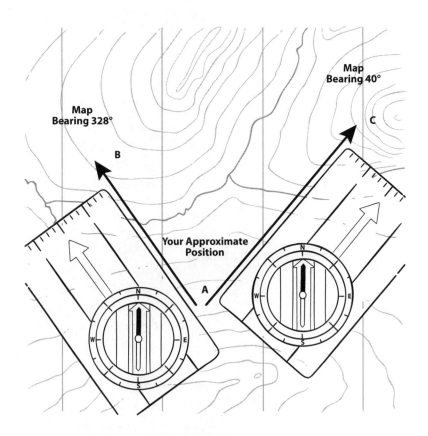

Resection

Here is a funny story that demonstrates just how easily folks get lost. I was in the woods one cold winter morning less than 200 yards from a main road where my vehicle was parked. After about thirty minutes I heard another vehicle drive up and park in close proximity to my own. I began to hear a crunch of snow coming from behind me; it did not sound like a deer but more like a human. As I sat in my stand I watched a hunter walk past me. He walked about 50 yards, then stopped, looked around, turned left and walked a few steps, and then he stopped and looked around again. After a couple of minutes he walked a few yards back to the right. At this point he began to look around him as though he was not sure exactly where he was; mind you, he was only 200 yards from a main road! After about ten minutes of wandering in what looked like small circles from my perch in the tree, he sat down by a tree, and I could tell he was not hunting—he was visibly fidgeting with his gear and acting like he was a bit nervous.

After a few minutes he began to walk again, but this time I coughed so as not to scare him too bad by calling out. When he looked in my direction I simply said, "You car is behind me about 200 yards." He replied, "I knew that," and walked off abruptly. Upon seeing my car, he should have known when he entered the woods that someone else might be about, and from his behavior I am certain he was lost within 200 yards of his car. In areas with lots of features that all look the same, like trees, one can become disoriented quickly. You should always take a bearing from where you start so you at least know the direction to return.

OBSTACLES

You may encounter many obstacles during your tramps, and you may have to either circumnavigate them or cross them. Circumnavigation of an object, such as a lake or pond, is pretty simple. You can choose to do one of two things, depending on the situation:

1. Find an easily identifiable object on the other side (if you can see that far) that is in the same line as the bearing you are traveling. Walk around and take another bearing from that object.

2. If you cannot see the other side of the obstacle, or there is no reliable way to identify something on the other side, then you will need to **90-90-90**. With this method, you will use your pace count. Stop at the edge of the obstacle, turn left or right 90°, and pace count until you get beyond the obstacle. Then, turn 90° forward, and walk until you have avoided the obstacle. If you are pace counting for distance, this leg needs to be recorded. Now turn 90° in the opposite direction, and walk the same number of paces you did on the first leg, creating a three-sided box. This will bring you back to the bearing you were on before encountering the obstacle.

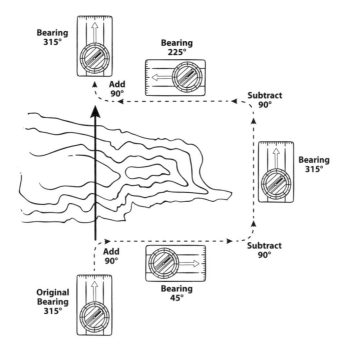

Obstacle

If you must cross an obstacle, it may be necessary to determine the distance across it. This might be true if you need to cut a tree for assistance in crossing, or if you have a rope and need to determine if it's long enough for a rope crossing.

1. Identify something that you can easily see on the other side of the obstacle.
2. At the edge of the obstacle, drive a stick into the ground directly in front of the object you identified.
3. Take a compass bearing to that object, turn left or right, and walk a straight line until you achieve a 45° difference with a compass reading from the original bearing to the same object. You have now created a right angle. The distance in paces back to your stake will be the same as the distance across the obstacle.

PAUL (POSITIVE AZIMUTH UNIFORM LAYOUT) METHOD

Using the **PAUL method** will allow you to scout an unknown area and figure a straight line bearing back to camp without backtracking by reverse azimuths all the way. This can come in very handy if you have covered quite a bit of distance. To use this method you will need to set up a log page in your journal for notes, and you will have to record bearings and distance to each point along the way. The easy way to accomplish this and still get your scouting done is to carry a flag or bandanna that is highly visible, preferably one that is orange.

Take an azimuth from your camp to a distant object. In your journal, record the azimuth and distance as you walk to it. Once you are there, place your flag on the object and continue scouting around the area—but never lose sight of the flag. When you are ready to move on, go back to the flag and take another reading to a distant object. Walk to it, recording the bearing and paces again in your journal. Place the flag on the object and scout around.

Continue this procedure until you are ready to return to camp. Draw a map in your book on a small scale, using the points and distances you have recorded. Decide the scale based on any measuring device—for example, 1" = 100 meters. Once you have drawn the map, (and this could easily be done with sticks on the ground or with rocks), check your return azimuth from the last point to your camp and the distance. You should then be able to travel back in a straight line. If you have camped along a creek or water source, you have a ready-made backstop.

FIGURING DAYLIGHT HOURS

There will be times when you want to know how much daylight you have left. It is prudent to set camp at least two hours before sunset in the summer and four hours in the winter, because of supplies needed for a comfortable night, such as wood. To figure this out without a watch, lift your hand up with your thumb tucked under and your fingers together. Place your hand under the sun. Every hand you can place between the sun and the horizon line going down equals one hour, and each finger represents fifteen minutes.

TIPS AND TRICKS FOR SUCCESSFUL NAVIGATION

1. **L.U.R.D.:** Left, Up, Right, Down. Remember that while the earth moves, it makes the objects in the sky move as well. Plant a stick in the ground and lie down on your back. Looking at the top of the stick like a gun sight, line this up with a star. After several minutes, the star will appear to have moved as the earth has rotated. If the star moves left, you are facing north. If the star moves up, you are facing east. If the star moves right, you are facing south. If it moves down, you are facing west. The movement can also occur in combination: Right and down

would be southwest. This method will work for any star except the North Star.

2. Remember that the moon travels in roughly the same arc as the sun, and at night makes a great navigational aid. It rises in the east and sets in the west, with its zenith hours of 10 P.M.–2 A.M. being in a southerly direction when you are looking at the moon.

3. A crescent moon can be used to easily find a southern direction in the Northern Hemisphere. An imaginary line drawn from the top crescent to the bottom of the crescent and to the horizon will indicate a southerly direction.

4. When traveling, it is always a good idea to look back at where you have been. On the return route, things will look more familiar if you have seen them from that angle before.

5. When using any method of navigation to get general direction other than a compass, check at least three methods for verification.

— Chapter 9 —

TREES:
THE FOUR-SEASON
RESOURCE

*"From the most ancient times, human beings have had
a primal belief that plants contain healing powers."*
—MATTHEW WOOD, *THE BOOK OF HERBAL WISDOM*, 1997

Since all plants have a growing season, many of the plants you
would use for anything from edibles to medicinal purposes have
a very short season in which to take advantage of them. Trees,
however, are a bit different; many of their resources are available
year round, the most important being construction materials and
medicines. By looking at common trees and the properties they
have, you can identify a few that will give you the greatest variety of resources. This chapter details the most important—and
resource-rich—trees that will be useful for your time in the bush.

PINES

Pines, being evergreens, keep their needles all year round, and
this can be a vital resource in the bush. White pine is the best for

medicinal value, and red pines are the best for other things such as fire-starting materials and construction tasks. All pines have edible seeds (although harvesting the nuts of most eastern species may be more trouble than it's worth). In the spring, young male cones (male cones are smaller and usually lower in the tree; they are usually coated in a dusty pollen and will never produce seeds) can also be eaten either raw or cooked, and the inner bark of pine is also palatable when separated into strips and fried crisp.

MEDICINAL VALUES

White pine needles can be made into an infusion very high in vitamin C that makes a good immune system–boosting drink. To accomplish this, collect a handful of needles, cut them in thirds, and place them into 8 ounces of boiled water. Place a lid on the container, and let them steep away from the fire for fifteen minutes. Strain and drink three times per day in winter or when food sources are scarce.

FIRST AID

Pine sap is a great resource for first aid as well as being an adhesive. In its raw form it can be used like a quick "new skin" plaster that will help cover a wound and is antiseptic. Pine sap can be found anywhere the tree has sustained injury. If it is needed and you can't find it, a purposeful cut to the tree with an axe will usually reveal a small amount fairly quickly. If you anticipate needing it over the long term, create areas along your route for future collection, using this same method.

Cut the outer bark from small branches into a strip to use as a makeshift plaster that is highly antiseptic and sticky on the inside as a result of the sap.

FIREWOOD

Fatwood is the resinous area of the pine tree that sap collects in naturally (see Chapter 7). Any area of the tree where a branch grows from the trunk will contain some fatwood. If the pine is dead standing, the sap will run to the base of the trunk and root areas. This fatwood can be identified by its thick appearance and feel when cutting, and will have a distinct turpentine smell. This wood is excellent fire-starting material and highly flammable both in fine shavings and in the form of feather sticks.

White pine also makes a decent kit for primitive fire-making, such as a bow drill set, but care must be taken to stay away from heavy resin-laden areas of deadwood for this task.

ADHESIVES

Pine pitch is made from a mixture of pine sap, charcoal from the fire, and some type of binder to give some flexibility, such as cattail head fibers or ground and powdered rabbit droppings. This makes a great adhesive for anything from patching containers to hafting an arrowhead or blade. The steps for making this mixture are as follows:

1. In a metal container, mix in the pine sap, charcoal, and binder material in equal parts.
2. Slowly heat and stir over a coal bed until it becomes a thick paste. Try not to let it catch fire, if possible, as this can make the pitch brittle.
3. Once the paste hardens, it can be stored. To reuse, heat it to the melting point.

Pine pitch works for making bandages, but remember that it will be hot, so be careful not to cause further injury with a burn. Once it is made, you can let it dry in the container and then reheat it when needed again. Or gather the pitch into pitch sticks for later use by turning a stick in the paste a bit at a time, like cotton candy, and allowing the pitch to dry on the stick. Reheat the hardened pitch until it softens and apply it in paste form.

BUILDING MATERIALS

Pine boughs are a great building recourse for many winter needs and can be used for bedding as well as shingling for shelters built from natural material. Remember that any bedding should be 4" thick compressed. When using plant materials for shingling, they should be interwoven so that they are upside down to the way they grow. This will create a shelter that sheds water, and resists water collection, preventing shelter leaks.

Pine and spruce pine roots make very passable cordages, especially for quick bindings and shelter building. You can find the roots just below the ground's surface and can pull them up in long sections. Pieces thinner than ⅜" will work best. If the outer bark of the root needs to be removed for better flexibility in your intended use, do this by pinching the root between two short sticks in the hand and pulling the root through. This vise will remove most of the bark.

WILLOWS AND POPLARS

These trees are all in the same family, and the four most common of these in the eastern woodlands are white and black willow, tulip poplar, and cottonwood. Poplars are some of the best trees for construction and combustion. All of these make excellent fire sets for primitive combustion (bow drill); all of them have inner barks that when dry can be processed into highly flammable bird's nests and tinder bundles.

Willow trees are very pliable, especially when young, and the bark makes great basket material and camp cooking implements. Because these woods are very soft, they make great carving materials for things such as bowls and spoons. In the summer, the barks can be removed in large pieces to create containers and quivers.

Willow bark has been used for thousands of years as a painkiller (like aspirin). It can be chewed, or you can prepare a decoction. See Appendix B for more information on making decoctions.

Willow is a great water indicator, as the trees require very moist soil to grow. Tulip poplar is among the tallest trees in the eastern woodlands, and because it drops its lower branches as it grows, it is a great place to seek fire-making materials. Other common trees in this family are saw tooth aspen, quaking aspen, and poplar.

BLACK WALNUT

Black walnut trees have many useful purposes and medicinal properties. We derive three main chemical compounds from this tree: iodine, tannin, and juglone.

- **Iodine** is a beneficial first-aid element for its ability to kill germs. In addition, it is what gives the black walnut its quality as a dye for anything from fabrics to wood to metal traps. (To effectively stain metal traps, boil them in a container with the green hulls of the black walnut tree.) The green hulls are also effective in preventing rust: when rubbed raw on metals such as 01 tool steel and 1095 knife blades, it will give them a nice dark patina that helps prevent rusting.
- **Tannin** is an astringent. The green leaves of this tree used in an infusion are excellent for drying conditions such as rashes and poison ivy. (See Appendix B for more information on making infusions.) Tannin also makes a great chemical for bark tanning hides. A cold solution of bark and hulls will yield a deep brown–colored hide that can be broken and worked after a few weeks of soaking.

- **Juglone** is a poison that prevents or stunts the growth of many plants, causing them not to grow well around the tree itself. It can also be used in a concentration for a fish-stunning potion if you use it in a restricted pool of water. Crush the black walnut hulls and place them in the water to release these toxins.

SASSAFRAS

The sassafras tree bark is a carminative (i.e., expels digestive gas) and will help with digestive disorders of any kind. It makes a pleasant tea, and it is also astringent and can be used as a poultice for skin ailments. The wood burns hot and long because of the inherent oils in the tree itself. Sassafras can be used as a dye for fabrics as well, yielding a rusty red color. This tree's bark and roots are also high in vitamin C, making it an immune-system booster.

NOTE: Check medicinal side effects before using internally.

OAKS

Oaks are some of the strongest of building material in the eastern woodlands; they make good bows and handles, and the wood burns long and hot. The medicinal value of oak cannot be overstated. There are two main types of oak: white and red. There is a simple way to tell the difference: Red oak has pointed leaves and white oak has lobed leaves. Red oak is the better of the two for construction purposes, and the white oak is better for medicines. White oak is such a powerful medicine that it was used as a symbol for the European *materia medica* for several hundred years. The inner bark of the white oak, when ground and decocted, is said to be good for all ailments above the neck. In addition, any type of fluid leakage can be controlled by this medicinal, from runny noses to diarrhea. Oaks are full of astringents and tannins.

These trees are considered the "model astringent" by authorities such as Matthew Wood. See Appendix B for information on making decoctions.

TIPS AND TRICKS FOR MAKING USE OF TREES

1. In the winter, you can simply cut through the bark of an oak to see if the inner bark is red or white, signifying red or white oak species.
2. If decoctions are not a feasible option, you can chew the bark to attain a similar effect.
3. Chewing pine resin like gum will cause excessive salivation and curb hunger pains, as well as ease a sore throat.
4. Do any medicinal collecting from the healthiest-looking live trees available.
5. Any infusion or decoction should be used in 8-ounce increments three or four times per day.

— Chapter 10 —

TRAPPING AND Processing Game

"The first thing to be considered in reference to a campaign is the selection of a trapping ground, and it is always desirable to choose a locality where travel by water can be resorted to as much as possible. Otter, mink, beaver, and muskrat are among the most desirable game for the trapper, and as these are all amphibious animals, a watered district is therefore the best on all accounts."

—W. HAMILTON GIBSON, *CAMP LIFE IN THE WOODS*, 1881

The art of trapping is much misunderstood. Think about hunting: You have the opportunity to scan for animals and with your chosen weapon shoot any creature that enters your kill range, which could easily be 100 or more yards. With a trap, you have to entice an animal to place its foot in a 2" circle when you are not even there. Trapping is as much an art form as tracking, but there are many ways to increase your chances of success. Once you have studied the concepts of sign and landscape tracking, it becomes a matter of understanding **sets** (trap placement), patience, and statistics. The more traps you set, the more chances you have of catching something. However, this does not mean you should set traps without a proper purpose. Pay attention to **setting signs**— that is, signs that animals have been in the area. Often, if you set a couple of traps near camp, you will not catch anything even in a few days, let alone overnight. Trapping is a game of percentages, and twelve traps should be a minimum number when considering this method to secure meat. I know that sounds like a lot, but it can be done with minimal materials in about an hour once you understand the basic principles.

UNDERSTANDING TRAP COMPONENTS

Almost all traps contain three major components: the **trigger**, the **lever**, and the **engine**:

1. The trigger is the part of the trap that actually gives way to set off the trap. In a primitive trap this is often the bait stick, or the wire triggers of a Conibear, for example.
2. The lever is usually the device that holds the tension employed by the trap and is released or moved by the trigger.
3. The engine is what powers the trap. It can be gravity in the case of the deadfall or the bent sapling of a green tree or bush. Anything that causes weight transfer or stores energy is an engine.

Traps are designed generally to perform one of three main functions: crush, strangle, or live capture. (Or, as John "Lofty" Wiseman put it, Strangle, Mangle, and Dangle.) The type of trap you set and its function will depend on the game you desire to trap. Remember that while live food never spoils, handling an angry raccoon can be a dangerous game, so discretion in trapping is always wise. It is better to kill the animal and be safe than to have to dispatch a possibly dangerous animal.

CREATING SIGN POSTS

The object of a sign post is to discover what animals are frequenting an area you plan to use for trapping. This step is not necessary if you have already found many signs and realize what you are after and what is in the area. To accomplish this is easy. Select a good area of possible frequent travel and set a stick in the ground. Clear the ground around this area for about 2' square so that tracks will be visible if an animal comes to investigate. Once this is set up, any type of visual or scent attractant can be used on the stick to bring animals in. A good practice is to use both types of attractants. For example, you can use the entrails of a frog and a feather or a bright piece of cloth tied to the stick. Animals will notice things that change on their daily routes, just as you would if someone moved something or placed something new in your living room. The animals come to investigate and leave tracks, enabling to you to identify what types of animals frequent the area. From this, you will better cater traps and baits for those animals.

BUSHCRAFT TIP

Scent control is overrated! Yes, I said overrated. It's not necessary to go overboard in controlling human odor. Mammals are curious, and they are all "sniffers"—they want to know what has been where and why, and some are even attracted to stinky things such as your sweat or urine. I know a guy who actually used the leaves he wiped himself with after defecating on his sign post, only to find it had attracted several raccoons and an opossum. Human odor can be very detrimental to hunting at times, but scavengers aren't bothered by it. The lesson here is, things that smell bad sometimes make the best attractant, and worrying about covering your scent is unnecessary. Dirt and a smoky fire will do a lot toward covering your scent as it is, and unless you have some foul-smelling chemical or fuel on your hands, you will be pretty safe.

BAIT FOR TRAPPING

Animals eat certain things; they also have favorite things, as well as new things they have not tasted but would surely like to, just like you and me. Finding these things can be easy or difficult depending on seasonality. For birds, nuts, seeds, and fruits are always a good bet; these also work well for small mammals such as chipmunks and squirrels. If you have something in your pack that is new and different that falls into this category, you may be ahead of the game.

A cashew nut may be new to squirrels, and the sweet aroma will definitely attract them. For other animals that are scavengers, such as raccoons or opossum, any stinky thing such as frog entrails or half of a bluegill will work well. The key element to good bait is finding something the animal wants that is not common to the area. If acorns are lying all over the ground, what is the chance a squirrel will pick the one that baits your tap? However, a lone walnut, broken to release the scent into the air, may be just the right ticket to attract the squirrel's attention. Birds like small fruit, so if you have to travel a bit to collect a few berries in an area where you know they are feeding on seed, you should do it!

MODERN TRAPS

The following section gives some basic uses for modern traps that I feel can be of the most benefit for a self-reliance-type kit. I do not cover all types of modern traps, only the ones that take up a small amount of space and are multifunctional. Modern traps are made of metal, so damage from animals or chew-outs (animals chewing through trap parts such as cordage snares) don't happen. These traps do take up space in your kit or pack and can be cumbersome in large numbers; carry about three of these in conjunction with steel cable snares and/or primitive trapping supplies.

THE #110 CONIBEAR

The **Conibear** trap (also called the "body grip"), named after its inventor, is probably the single most effective trap ever made. It has the capability to take all small game species, including water fowl, ground birds, and even fish, with a proper set. It is a killing trap, and very seldom will animals be found alive in it. It can be set to differing sensitivity levels and can be used baited or set with no bait. You can easily set the smaller #110 by hand, where the #220 is normally set using a tool, making it a less than optimum option.

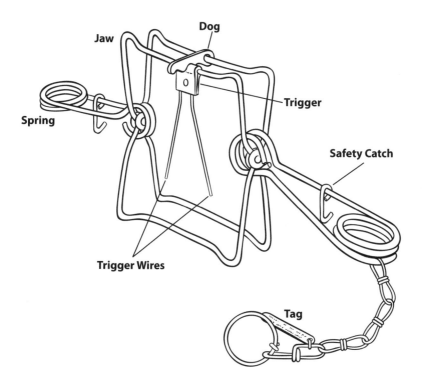

Body grip trap

CABLE SNARES

As the term implies, **cable snares** are snares made from steel cable. Their size depends on your quarry. Usually cable snares have mechanisms called locks that prevent the snare from loosening, so the more the animal struggles, the tighter the snare. This may seem inhumane, but it can kill the animal quickly.

A trap or snare engine is a device to activate the trap quickly, instead of relying on the animal's attempted escape to tighten the noose. An engine can be a springy green branch, a counterweight, or a shock cord of some sort; it is only limited by your imagination. Cable snares are a good way to carry many traps without sacrificing a lot of weight, especially if they are of minimum size. These can also be fashioned from common materials. The only downside to snares is that they will most likely be useful only once—if an animal is caught, the snare will be twisted and kinked to a point of uselessness.

Snare

IMPROVISED TRAPPING MATERIALS

You can use many materials to improvise modern traps or those made from non-cordage materials:

1. Picture-hanging wire obtained at any hardware store works well for making cable snares capable of taking rabbit-size game with ease. #4 wire is best for this task. One thing to remember when using wire is that small-gauge wire, when incorporated with an engine, can sever flesh or decapitate your prey.

2. Guitar strings also make good cable snares, as long as you use the heavier-wound strings and not the thinner single-wire strings.

3. Simple steel leaders used for fishing are a ready-made snare with simple adjustment, and will serve two purposes if carried—fishing and trapping.

4. Rat traps are an often overlooked asset to a small trapping kit and are like a poor man's Conibear: very effective for smaller animals up to squirrels and small birds. When using rat traps for trapping, paint them a dull, earth-toned color and drill a hole in one corner to anchor them and keep them from being dragged away in case of a non-killing strike.

THE BASICS OF UPLAND TRAPPING

Upland trapping refers to setting traps above the water on higher ground for animals such as coyote, fox, raccoon, opossum, and other small land animals. Depending on the type of traps you are using and game you are seeking to trap, setting traps on land requires a bit more equipment than water trapping. For the purpose of this section, we will only discuss foothold traps; later we'll talk about snares and body grip traps.

A **foothold trap** is one in which the animal is held fast, generally by the foot, and remains alive until arrival of the trapper. There are five main components to such traps:

1. The **frame**. This is the base of the trap to which all other components are attached.
2. The **spring(s)**. These can be long spring(s) or coil spring(s); these operate the jaws to close them.
3. The **jaws**. They are generally made of steel and are either offset or not offset, meaning that there is a space cut out so that the jaws have a bit of gap in the closed position. (This aids in the animal's comfort and help prevent "ring offs"—situations in which the animal's leg is cut off because of its struggles to escape the trap jaws.)
4. The **pan**. This is the target area where you want the animal to place the full weight of its front foot when it approaches the bait.
5. The **dog**. This is the level that holds the tension of the trap jaws. When the animal steps on the pan, this releases the dog, which lies over what is called the operating or "strong" jaw of the trap and is toggled in a catch notch on the pan.

There are three basic types of foothold traps used for upland set: the **single spring, double spring,** and **coil spring**.

A single "long" spring trap is a set of steel jaws that are closed by one power spring when the pan is tripped. A double long spring has two springs operating the jaws, and a coil spring can be single or double as well. A coil spring, as you might expect, is a spring made of a coiled piece of metal wire. In the days of old the mountain trappers carried mainly long spring traps and these are what are most familiar in image to non-trappers.

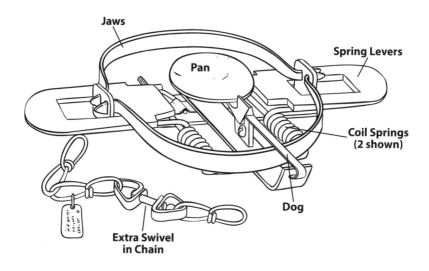

Coil spring trap

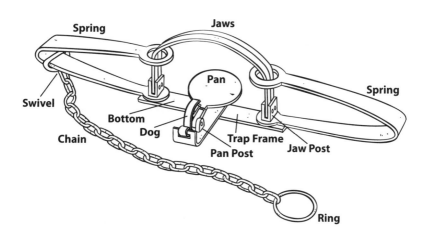

Long spring trap

Before we get the traps ready for use we need to speak about another important item: **Pan tension** refers to the amount of downward pressure required to move the pan down and release the dog. In newer traps, this is controlled by a screw attaching the pan to the trap frame. Tightening this screw will make the pan more difficult to move; the reverse holds true if it is loosened. Pan tension determines what type of animals you catch— it will take a heavier animal to release a trap with more pan tension, thus helping to reduce the chances you'll capture a nontarget animal.

Attached to the frame of the trap is the trap chain. This is usually connected to a stake or anchor to keep the trapped animal from running away with the trap. The length of chain varies; I prefer about 18" of chain and at least three swiveling points. Swivels will help keep the animal from twisting the chain and further injuring itself while awaiting your arrival.

PREPARING YOUR TRAPS

Let's get our traps ready for use. When traps come from the factory, they are coated with oil to keep them from rusting in transport or storage. This oil must be removed so that the trap can be dyed or waxed or both. To remove this oil, boil the traps in hot water and then let them air dry until they lightly rust. Yes, you want them to get a light coat of rust, as the dyes and waxes will stick to the metal better that way. Once the traps are cleaned of any oil, they can be dyed with commercial products or boiled in black walnut hulls.

COMPANION EQUIPMENT FOR YOUR TRAPS

As with any other hobby, there are a lot of trap-related gadgets on the market, but you can (and should) keep things simple. You will need a screen to sift fine granules of dirt onto your set. For pounding stakes, the hammer pole of an axe will do, or even a large batoning log. For digging the trap bed, an E-tool (entrenching tool), small hand trowel, or even a digging stick will work fine. A small brush for exposing the pan is very helpful, but I have found that blowing the pan off to expose it has no ill effect on the catch.

> **BUSHCRAFT TIP**
>
> A word on waxing traps: The reason you do so is to help them operate smoothly, as well as keep further rust from forming. It will also keep them operating if you use them in water or wet ground in freezing temperatures. The best wax for this operation is beeswax; you can buy it commercially if you don't have a homegrown supply. Dying the trap is not absolutely necessary; according to many experts, spray paint or nothing will work as well. As long as the trap is well lubricated with wax, it will operate and catch animals if properly set.

STAKING THE TRAPS

You will need large stakes or earth anchors to hold your traps in place. The two preferred methods for this are **rebar stakes**, about 2' long, or **earth anchors**. An earth anchor is a piece of angle metal attached to a cable. When driven into the ground, it goes straight, but when pulled upward it will turn sideways in the dirt below, anchoring the trap fast. I have met many old trappers who used wooden stakes to trap with. These can be fashioned from natural material easily enough, although this will force you to carry strong wire (16-gauge minimum) with which to attach the traps to the stakes. The main problem with earth anchors is that they are difficult to remove without a large levering device. However, using them ensures that your catch won't get away from you, nor will you lose your trap. All traps not secured by an earth anchor should be double staked.

Trail set

TRAP SETUP

With your equipment in hand, you are ready to set your traps. Remember, as with all real estate, the key is location, location, location! A trap set in the wrong place will usually not catch or will take longer to catch than one placed in a good spot. Most game travels on specific trails or routes, and these places are the best for your traps.

To begin with, look for signs that animals are there; tracks, scat, and refuse from feeding are all good indicators. Anywhere trails meet or connect is prime location in a wooded environment. At intersections I like to set two traps at 45° from one another on opposite sides of the trail. The old saying goes, "If it was good enough to set one trap, it's good enough to set two."

You can set traps where trails meet open fields. High ground is generally preferred to low ground in open areas, as most predatory animals travel higher for good visibility to detect prey. When selecting your trap location, be sure to account for the wind; any bait or lure you are using to attract an animal will need to be upwind so that the smell travels well.

BAITING TRAPS

Baiting a trap is a key element to the setting of it. Most of the time you will want the animal to work to get the bait. Bait set on the trigger system of a trap, unless placed in a tray-style mechanism, should be attached to the triggering device so that it cannot be taken easily. In other sets, just placing the bait as far as possible to the rear of the trap can be effective enough to force the animal to trigger the trap. You want the animal to work for the bait as you are trying to trap him; you don't want to feed him!

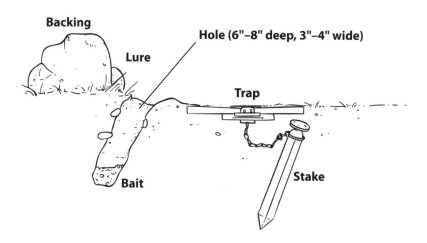

Dirt hole trap

MOST BAIT CAN BE FOOD

Remember that unless you are using pieces of other kills that you are not eating, such as entrails, most bait you use is also food that can be eaten to serve as nourishment for your body. The point to remember is this: How much bait do you have to use proportional to the amount of protein you'll derive from the trapped animal? If you're expending more energy to capture food than you're getting from it, you need to find another way of getting something to eat.

Another lesson I try to instill in all my students: Don't wait until you are hungry to secure food; this will only make things worse and lessen the chance for success. Just like anything else, hunting, fishing, and trapping use calories and energy. If you wait till the tank is empty, you won't have the resources to make your hunting efficient. One of the greatest benefits to attempting to find food in the wild is the fact that it occupies the mind. This can work wonders in times of waiting in an SAR (Search and Rescue) scenario.

Does all this mean that you should not eat the legs from a large frog before using the rest of the uneaten bits for baiting a trap? Of course not; it means that you should pick and choose what you eat and conserve resources when you can for bigger meals, taking easy, high-protein, high-fat foods and using the other things to obtain more protein and fat. Always look to better your situation; that is what survivability is all about. Smooth it, don't rough it!

BUSHCRAFT TIP

The difference between baits and lures is simple: a **lure** attracts the animal by smell to the set location, and **bait** is something the animal wants to eat or investigate. Lures are usually made of glands or oils, and bait is usually food based. A good example of lure is skunk musk; it can bring animals in for a look from a very long distance. Bait consists of things such as raw meat.

TRAP SPECIFICS

With a good location selected, you must decide how large or small the trap should be and what trap to use. For leg-hold traps I prefer double long spring (DLS) traps. A small DLS will hold the same animals that a larger single spring will hold, but it will also catch smaller game. These traps are much more stable for water sets and generally safer as well as easier to set than single spring or coil spring traps. I prefer the #11 DLS made by Sleepy Creek. I have caught everything from opossum and raccoon to coyote in it.

I recommend carrying at least six of these in conjunction with snares and body grips, but three will suffice if weight is an issue. For longer-term meat and fur gathering, twelve would be better, but to carry that many traps you will need transport other than just a pack. For good all-around meat-gathering trapping, I carry no more than twelve traps in any combination. Carrying the right twelve traps for your environment will keep you in meat without hunting anything if you set them right.

Gloves, incidentally, are not necessary when trapping unless you are worried about safety. I find they are dangerous when setting my traps since they inhibit feeling in my fingers, which I rely on to set a trap safely.

DIGGING A TRAP BED

When you are ready to set your trap in a great location that will attract even the most wary of animals, begin by digging a **trap bed**. This is the area that conceals your trap so that the set looks natural. The bed must be deep enough to cover your stakes or anchors as well as the trap chain; insert these first and cover them before the trap is actually bedded on top of them. Bedding the trap is one of the most important steps in trapping. Believe it or not, if you create a perfect set with an imperfectly bedded trap, you'll wind up with your trap face down, still set, on top of the dirt. If the trap is not bedded solidly, it will rock in the dirt. When an animal is working your set and accidently steps on the outer or weak jaw of the trap, this causes the strong jaw to rise up in the dirt. This arouses the animal's curiosity and it will dig where the movement occurred, generally hooking the jaw of the trap and pulling it up. The game is over at that point.

The #11 DLS trap has two springs that act as stabilizers. Thus even if the bedding is not perfect, the trap does not rock nearly as easily as the coil spring trap.

Make sure the trap is properly bedded first, always according to the wind direction and with the dog toward the back of the set. This prevents the dog from blocking the animal's foot or pushing it out of the way of the closing jaws. After the trap is set and covered with sifted dirt, continue to cover the entire trap bed with sifted dirt. This is important because you do not want large clumps of dirt, debris, or rocks affecting the trap's operation or jamming within the jaws, causing separation and escape of the animal. Once you have completed the bedding, sweep lightly or blow off the dirt from your pan to expose it to view. This step helps you decide offset (the relationship of the pan to the actual dirt hole or baited area) and where your backing and dirt hole/visual attractants will be placed.

CREATE YOUR BACKING

Backing is the structure behind the set that prevents the animal from approaching from any direction but where you want it to come from. It can be anything from a semicircle of dirt, leaves, or other debris, to a log, tree, rock, or stump. Place a dirt hole against the backing to serve as a bait holder. The hole should be approximately 12" deep at a 30–45° angle. This does two things:

1. It forces the animal to approach from the front to get his eyes and nose in line with the hole.
2. It forces the animal to go deep to find the prize or dig—either way is fine.

Within the hole place some sort of attractant; there are many commercial baits on the market, of course, but you can use anything that stinks. I prefer Catfish Sticky bait, which comes in a large container; it lasts a long time, and a little is all you need. As an alternative, anything that is left from the last kill will do fine. Just think stinky—anything rotten will work.

> **BUSHCRAFT TIP**
>
> Another great trick for the dirt hole is to bait the hole and then plug it with the tail from another kill, such as a rabbit or raccoon. This becomes a visual attractant as well. Remember that animals hunt by sight and smell, so visuals are always a good addition. Sometimes they alone are enough. Another technique is to use a prominent feature as the backing. This could be a large bone, burnt log, or anything that directly contrasts with the environment to attract animals visually to the set.
>
> Bait or lure the item itself. You can shove bait into the bone cavities or even just place some guts under a large rock covered with a bit of dirt to seem as though it was buried by another animal. The object is to make the animal approach your trap from the front and stick its nose in the hole to work the set; this is where offset comes into play.

OFFSET

Offset is both left to right and front to back. Think about the animal: He leads with one foot, and it will be offset from centerline. You can force which foot that is by fencing. (We will talk about this shortly.) The size of the critter dictates how far the distance is from his nose to his foot. I have many times made a rear-leg catch on a smaller animal such as a fox or raccoon when attempting to set for coyote with a larger back set. I have found that for trapping of meat, a small 2–4" offset in both directions works best. If you're attempting to trap larger predators, you will need a 6–9" offset.

FINAL STEPS

Once you decide your offset and are able to see exactly where your pan is, set up your dirt hole or visual attractant or both. Then place your backing if it is not a naturally occurring object. Once the backing is in place, you can worry about fencing.

Fencing is what you use to make the animal put its foot exactly where you want it to be. It can be very simple, such as some of the rough material from your sifter, which the animal will not want to step on. Try not to make any fencing or backing extend beyond the front or "loose" jaw of the trap. It will make the animal wary of placing its foot into the confined space if it extends beyond the trap jaws. In other words, for the jaw opposite the dog, there is such a thing as "too much fencing." You can then use secondary fencing, such as pebbles, sticks, and even chaff, to crowd the animal further toward the pan.

Once all these steps are complete, lightly cover the pan with sifted dirt; about ¼" is plenty. By this time, the pan should be the lowest part of the entire set. That is what you want because the animal will have to put its weight down to step there comfortably. When the set is complete, you can then bait, lure, place visuals, or all three. Scat from other animals is always a good curiosity booster, serving as a visual and olfactory attractant, as well as secondary fencing. Feathers placed into a dirt backing make a great visual attractant as well. A great teacher once told me that every set should have a BLT: "Bait, Lure, and a Turd."

WATER TRAPPING

Land animals, in general, have fur worth more money but water mammals are much easier to catch and thus are a more reliable source of meat. Water trapping requires less finesse and less equipment than trapping land animals, and the bait will be readily available in the water or on the water's edge.

Simplicity is the name of the game here. Most of the animals in those areas are amphibious and are related to rats, so they are not that intelligent compared to canine and feline species. You will do well trapping in the water with a few double long spring traps from #1 to #3 sizes. With them you can catch mink and beaver.

Water sets require no bedding, as the water is your trap bed and the long springs will make stability a nonissue. The main sets used for water trapping are a **pocket set** or a **castor mound set** for beaver.

POCKET SET

A pocket set is a hole pushed into the bank, which you can make with the toe of your boot. Place the bait in the hole, the hole being just above water level, and center the trap on the hole. You can use fencing as well; set up a few sticks to direct the animal in from the front, forcing it to step on the trap pan.

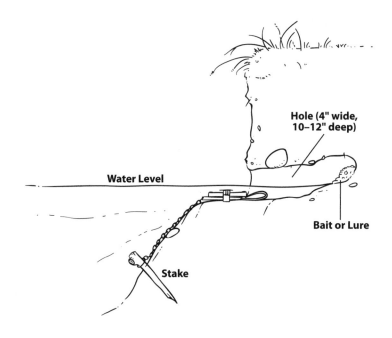

Pocket set

CASTOR MOUND SET

For beaver, the best sets are called castor mounds. If you can catch one beaver, the castor yielded will catch the next, and the next, and so on. Castor is produced as a scent by a beaver to mark territory; there are castor glands near the base of its tail. This is a very attractive scent to all animals but especially attractive to other beaver.

Create a shelf at the edge of the bank to set a #3 double long spring trap about 10–12" deep in the water on the shelf, and offset about ½ the distance from one side to center to one side of center, left or right. On the bank, create a false slide by dragging your foot through the mud, as if a beaver has slid into the water on his belly. If you can find a genuine fresh slide, set the trap here, as this may not require baiting with castor. Above the slide, place some fresh torn grasses and a few sticks you have freshly whittled. Place some castor on this pile if you have it. Beavers will constantly patrol the edges of the water and investigate these slides. As one bellies up to the bank, it will drop its foot into your trap.

Muskrats are very much like beaver, but if you can find a lodge or slide signaling their presence, these are also ideal places to use small #110 Conibears. Mink are carnivores, and muskrat is their favorite meal, so any muskrat meat you don't eat should be used for this. Raccoons and possum patrol the banks as well, and any rotten fish or smelly material will attract their attention.

Just as with fishing, large traps with heavy pan tension catch large animals; small traps with light pan tension will catch about any animal.

SPECIALTY SETS

In addition to the sets discussed earlier, there are some specialty sets. In this category, I would place one blind set (that is, set without bait) that you can create with wire snares: the **squirrel pole set**. Using this method, you set up an avenue or path of least resistance for the squirrel by leaning a fallen tree against another in which the animals are already living or are frequenting. They will invariably travel up this pole rather than climb up the main trunk of the tree. Using a series of open snares on this bridge will yield squirrels nine times out of ten. You can even drive the animals into the trap by spooking them off the ground to the trees.

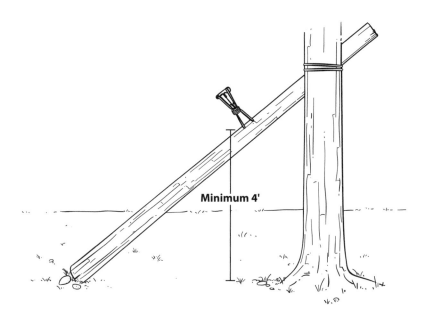

Minimum 4'

Leaning pole trap

PRIMITIVE TRAPPING

Primitive traps have been used by ancient peoples since we became hunter-gatherers, and they are just as effective today as they were in ancient times. The biggest advantage to primitive trapping is that it takes a lot less gear carried to accomplish, and setup time is minimal once you own the skills. You can set a trap line of twenty traps in a matter of an hour once you are familiar with the system and used to doing it. This takes practice and dirt time just like any other skill, but it is as important an ability as fire-starting or shelter building.

TRIGGERS

The most important thing to learn in simple primitive trapping is one trigger system that can be adapted to many traps. In this way, you can pre-make several snares and adjust triggers and traps on the fly to fit the situation. A simple toggle trigger is all you need to set a variety of traps that will catch all small game, as well as birds and even fish for bank line sets. It is much better to be familiar with a few traps that employ this simple trigger than to have some knowledge of many complicated traps that require time and energy to employ. Carving complicated components takes time and much thought as well as adjustment to make them right, whereas straightforward toggles are just that simple, and many of these traps can be made using no tools at all. For every complicated trap you set, you can set many simple traps and obtain the same, or better, results.

> **BUSHCRAFT TIP**
>
> Many people overcomplicate primitive trapping! Trapping is very simple to understand. Any trap that effectively holds or kills an animal is all you need. I have traveled all over the world, and tribal people who are still hunter-gatherers have shown me that simple traps employing a simple toggle trigger are the best all-around trap to use for securing meat, and the ones they use every day for small mammals and birds. The KISS (keep it simple and sensible) method works for trapping.

DEADFALL TRAPS

Deadfall traps have been employed for centuries, most often used on smaller game such as ground squirrels, mice, and larger rodents. Deadfall traps can be used with the same toggle-trigger system used for snare traps. This is called the "**Paiute deadfall**" after the desert Paiute Indians, who used it quite frequently. Deadfall traps need to be five times heavier than the prey to be killed; the trap will crush the prey. However, that does not mean the animal will be instantly killed—it may suffocate over time.

You can add combinations, such as a **cubby set**. Cubby sets are small holes like pocket sets sometimes used at the base of a tree or log. They are built over a deadfall trap to add weight to the trap and help disguise it to make it more effective. Traditional Paiute deadfalls employed large rocks as the killing device. You can adapt this trap to woodland areas using logs or the previously mentioned cubby set. Other deadfall traps for medium animals can be easily fashioned to employ larger logs by building a simple frame, yet using the same toggle trigger. These traps are limited only by your personal ingenuity. The main disadvantage to this trap system is the availability of component parts depending on where you are, and the time needed to build them.

BIRD TRAPS

Bird traps can employ the same snare-and-toggle system previously discussed, or they can be cage traps deployed to catch the bird alive, conserving it for later use. Many cage traps are used for smaller birds, but larger birds and waterfowl are better trapped using other methods, as discussed in the preceding sections. Cage traps work well for ground-dwelling birds such as quail, grouse, and pheasant. They can also be used for small perching species such as mourning doves and turtledoves.

Using a snare device to catch birds does not require the tensile strength needed for small mammals, so carrying multi-ply cordage that can be broken down in diameter is a big plus when trapping birds in this fashion. A breakaway toggle system is used for these type of traps and can be adapted to deadfalls as well. The system for live bird trapping usually employs a trip wire or stick of sorts, forcing the bird to cross it to get to bait.

SMALL TRAPPING KITS

Trapping kits can range from elaborate to a roll of **bank line** (tarred nylon used for fishing and net-making) and a knife. I prefer the light weight of a small kit, relying on my knowledge and skill to employ a lot of traps. I carry a few items to help ensure success while keeping weight and space to a minimum.

There is something to be said for the bank-line-and-knife-only kit. The main additions I suggest for a short-term situation or an emergency kit for your pack are a couple of medium treble hooks (again, multipurpose for trapping and fishing), a half-dozen larger barrel sinkers, and large single hooks in a plastic zip-lock bag contained inside the roll of bank line, held in by a couple of corks and a roll of #4 picture wire. The main use for the wire is for special traps such as squirrel poles where you need the rigidity of wire over bank line. It adds little weight and can be multi-use as a steel leader for limb sets and fishing if turtles are prevalent. Limb sets involve hanging a baited line from a limb with a hook on the end under water. For fishing, add a pocket fishing kit.

FISHING WITH IMPROVISED RODS AND TENKARA

Some of the best fishing rods are made from bamboo or river cane. These can be anywhere from 9' to 13' in length, and cutting them green will work fine. Lines for rods of this nature should be the same length as the rod. No need to reel in the line—use the leverage of the rod to bring the fish within distance of the dip net or bank to secure the catch.

DISCOVER TENKARA

The fishing technique called "**tenkara**" is used in the mountains of Japan and has now started to spread rapidly to other parts of the world. It is based on the same concepts as cane pole fishing, with some adaptations. Tenkara is used mainly in rivers and streams, so it is a form of fly fishing and not far from dapping (lifting a lure/fly up and dropping it back down on the water's surface, jigging it on top the water). The brilliance of tenkara is the way lines and riggings are attached and detached from the rod. You can have several different rigged lines for different applications, which you can attach and detach from the rod within a few seconds without having to cut or tie a line to or from the rod. You do this by using what's called a lillian braid attached to the end of your rod. This can easily be fashioned from the mantle of any parachute cord or small-diameter cordage:

1. Using a piece of para cord approximately 3" long, slide the end of the cord over the end of your rod as if it were a stocking.
2. Leave about 2" of this overhanging and attach the first 1" permanently by wrapping the rod at that point with small-diameter string or line. Seal this with pine resin so it forms a bond to the rod.
3. Tie a knot in the mantle at the very end and burn this nylon material a bit to create a sort of ball on the end. Once this is accomplished, your rod is now ready to accept any rigged lines.

RIGGING LINES

As stated earlier, with a tenkara pole you can keep multiple rigged lines to match fishing conditions and quickly change them out to adjust. You can have floating fly lines, braided lines, and furled lines on different storage ladders rigged with different lures and hook combinations as well. Generally, carrying four different rigged lines will allow you to cover most scenarios. After you have chosen the type of line and rigging for that particular line (e.g., hooks, sinker, float or dry fly, and strike indicator), tie a simple loop in the top of the line using a figure 8 with a ½" loop. To attach the lines to your rod, create a lark's head loop in the line and place that over the ball knot you created on the lillian braid. At that point, it will self-tighten. It won't come off but will be easy to remove when you want to change lines.

BUSHCRAFT TIP

Line ladders are keepers to hold the rigged lines neatly and are not absolutely necessary. The lines can be coiled into a tin if you desire, but the ladders will keep them from getting knotted when removed for use. A ladder is simply a miniature of a ladder made from wood or plastic. They can be easily fashioned from a flat strip of wood carved into a half-moon shape on each end. The length is a matter of personal preference; I like mine about 4" long. Wrap the line around them to keep it neat for use and set up for that particular application.

PROCESSING SMALL GAME

Processing small game is faster and easier than processing a large animal and requires less energy to transfer the meat back to camp from the area of kill or capture. The main reason for concentrating on small game, though, is that many times it can be consumed in one setting, leaving some leftovers for bait. To process and cook or preserve large game is a time-consuming and sometimes tedious undertaking. In areas where predatory animals are present, having large amounts of meat, blood, or carcasses in your camp area can be very dangerous. Processing small game is a very easy task for the most part and can be accomplished by anyone with minimal skill or practice.

SMALL MAMMALS

Many smaller mammals such as ground squirrels, mice, rats, and the like need no processing other than making a shallow slice to remove guts and anal tract. You can then place them in the fire to burn the fur off and cook the meat. Consume them whole to get all the nutrients from a small meal. Remember that any leftover meat should be used for baiting a trap to catch something else.

MEDIUM-SIZE MAMMALS

Medium-size critters are not that much more difficult to handle; you just need to remove the fur to make them easy to process, and quarter them for quicker cooking. Remove all innards and the anal tract. Be careful not to perforate the gut or intestines while removing them, as this can foul the taste of the meat. Many innards are worth consuming, such as the heart and liver. Check the organs of any kill to ensure that they look healthy: brightly colored with no blotching or worms. Again, remember to use leftovers for several traps or fishing.

PROCESSING OTHER GAME

The eastern woodlands offer a wide variety of other game that can sustain you if you know how to trap and prepare it.

BIRDS

Removing or plucking the feathers in the wild can be a time-consuming process; you are better off skinning the bird as you would a mammal. The main thing to remember with birds is to empty the **crop**, a pouch at the base of the throat where food is held prior to digestion. This will usually contain dry seeds and such from recent feedings. Again, livers and hearts make great food, and all birds are edible. However, with scavenger birds such as buzzards, you should boil the meat well to ensure that any parasites are killed prior to consumption. Use your best judgment when examining the meat and organs for overall health.

FISH

Process fish by slitting them from the vent or anus to the base of the gills, removing all guts, and tearing out the gills. You can scale the fish or just cook it with the scales or skin on, and eat the meat from the inside out like a baked potato. If you choose to skin a catfish before eating, you will want a pair of pliers for scaling and skinning, as it can be tough. All freshwater fish in North America are edible.

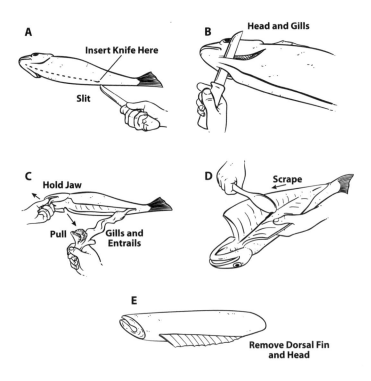

How to clean fish

REPTILES AND AMPHIBIANS

Reptiles such as snakes can be skinned and the guts removed, then cooked like any other food. Remove the head of any poisonous snake prior to processing. Frogs can also be skinned or just cooked and consumed after gutting. Turtles are a bit tricky: Cut the head off, hang the body upside down to bleed out, remove the lower shell by cutting the thin layer of membrane between the shell and the meat, and clean out the innards. You can use the shell as a pot in which to cook the meat. Turtle meat makes very good bait for fishing.

PRESERVING MEAT

Since ancient times humans have preserved meat for later use. There are many ways of doing this. Here are a few simple ways you can preserve with little to no excess gear or additional resources.

DRYING

Drying removes moisture from the meat and makes it available for consumption later on a trip or on the trail. The key is to cut the meat as thin as possible so that the process happens quickly. You can dry meat in several different ways depending on natural resources available to you.

❑ Suspend the meat over a fire with low heat for a period of time until the meat cracks when bent, like jerky.
❑ Sun-dry the meat on a flat rock or rack. If a full hot sun is available, rotate the meat from side to side until dry.

The meat can also be smoked while drying to add flavor and additional bacteria-killing agents. Note that this is not the same process as smoking meat (discussed in the next section).

SMOKING

To smoke meat, you will need an enclosure of some sort made from available gear such as a poncho, trash bag, space blanket, etc. It can also be made from natural material. Build a tripod with a rack for smoking the meat approximately 2' above a hot bed of coals and small flame. The enclosure causes the smoke and heat to rise directly to the meat and accomplishes the smoking process. Unlike with drying, you are actually slow cooking the meat and not trying to remove all moisture. The smoke adds flavor as well as antibacterial properties to the meat. You can use green wood to aid in smoke content, but stay away from resinous woods such as pines.

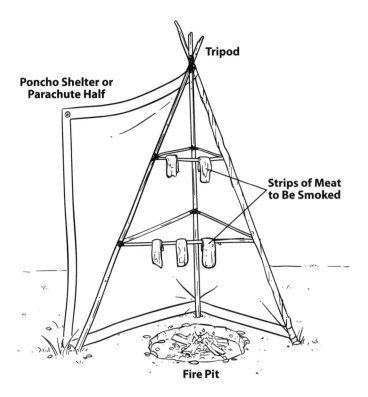

Smoking meat

TIPS AND TRICKS FOR SUCCESSFUL TRAPPING

1. Rotten and fishy meat attract scavenger-type animals.
2. Cats hunt more by sight than by smell, so hanging visuals above the set works best if you're trapping felines.
3. Canine predators will be more attracted to meat baits in the winter when other food is scarce.
4. Skunks that are shot then bagged in a drum liner can be used to contaminate other items with scent.
5. Skunk scent is one of the best long-distance call lures.
6. Beaver castor will attract almost *all* animals.

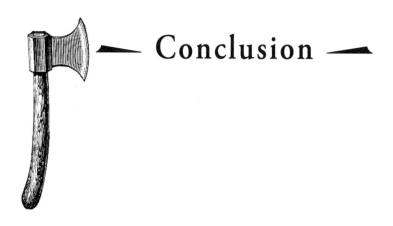

Conclusion

I would like to thank you for reading this book. Of course, it's important that you not only absorb its lessons but also get outside and enjoy what nature has to offer. The best way to learn the skills we've discussed is to practice them.

It is important that we not forget the teachings of our forefathers and that we pass on these skills to those who wish to learn. While we are all bushcrafters and woodsmen at heart, we must also remember that we are stewards of the land. Conservation of resources and keeping things renewable and renewed should be a main goal on any outing. Only in this way will there be beautiful areas of the land for our children and their children to enjoy.

It's possible that when you venture into the wild something will go wrong. In that case, practicing these bushcrafting skills on shorter, easier tramps will help prepare you to better handle an emergency. Rather than face a life-and-death situation, you'll be able to turn it into a serious but not deadly problem, one that's capable of solution.

It has taken me years of research and experiment to discern which are the most valuable skills to own and which are the most important items to carry. This book is an attempt to sum that up in a short space and with a few illustrations. Volumes could be written on individual topics, but I also believe in the 80/20 rule of life: 80 percent of what you hear and see on a daily basis is the least valuable information. This book covers what I believe to be the 20 percent of bushcraft that is of the most value. It will not only make you a better bushcrafter, but it will allow you to "smooth it" rather than rough it.

And in the end, that's what counts. Good luck!

Appendix A

THE PATHFINDER CONCEPT:
Conserving
AND
Utilizing
Resources

Conserving resources means many things. In the context of this book, it means the need to be frugal and make the greatest use possible of the resources you have. If you're stranded in the wild, you don't know how long it will be before you're found, so you must understand and conserve key resources. Here are some things to get you thinking.

TEN THINGS TO REMEMBER

1. Never use your knife unless you have to. Break sticks whenever possible, and strip bark by hand or with sharp rocks.
2. Never pass an opportunity to collect dry tinder for later use. Start fires with primitive methods if you have time and calories to burn, and save the sure flame for when you absolutely need it.
3. Never waste meat after securing it. Dry whatever you have left and store it in a bandanna for later consumption.
4. Make use of all parts of any animal. Bones can make tools and innards can be used for bait.
5. Use deadfall for shelters and fires whenever possible to avoid wasting energy breaking and cutting materials.
6. Water can be precious. Whenever rain is imminent, set up a collection device.
7. Do not travel unnecessarily to secure game. Run traps in a daisy pattern around your base camp instead of a line.
8. Set up your camp near water when possible. This makes collection of water and securing food more accessible and requires less travel.
9. Always think about the next fire and plan it by making char cloth or sparing some tinder.
10. Travel during times of easy comfort. In hot weather, travel in the mornings and evenings, and in cold weather travel during times of high sun.

Appendix B
WILD EDIBLES
AND
Medicinal Plants

Too many people get wrapped up in identifying wild edibles and what they can and cannot eat. Again, keep it simple. Look around your yard; there are probably several very common wild edible plants. Instead of worrying about the plants that are few and far between, concentrate on the common ones. Pick eight, then commit them to memory. On a recent trip to New Zealand, I was astonished to see that many of the same plants that are in the United States are also thriving there; dandelions, clover, plantains, cattails, etc., were all growing just as they do here. Chances are, if you spend much time in the wild, you'll become lost or stranded at least once, so concentrate on common plants. If you can identify eight edible plants, at least a few will be common in other areas of the United States, as well as abroad. You can do yourself a great service by learning families of plants so that you can identify edibles by similarity. However, be aware that many plants have poison look-alikes. **Warning:** Never eat wild mushrooms or any other fungi. Fully identify any plant before consuming it.

There are four groups of edibles that provide good nutritional value but not fat. You should memorize at least two in each group and learn to recognize the tree or plant in all seasons.

1. Starches, Roots, and Tubers
2. Fruits and Berries
3. Nuts
4. Greens

The following is a list of some common edibles from these categories:

EDIBLES	CATEGORIES
Cattail	Roots/Tubers
Parsnip	Root (Warning: This plant's leaves and stem may cause contact dermatitis.)
Dandelion	Greens
Burdock	Greens/Roots
Hickory	Nut
Walnut	Nut
Raspberry/Blackberry/Salmon Berry	Fruit
Common Elderberry	Fruit

- **Cattails** are nature's supermarket and pharmacy. The young shoots are edible raw or boiled; the root stock tubers can be boiled and eaten as well. The pollen collected from the seed heads can be used as flour, and the young seed heads can be eaten like corn on the cob.
- **Field parsnip** was used as a staple food for centuries, but is now forgotten by most; the root of this plant is a great starch and can be baked like a potato. Warning: Contact dermatitis can occur when handling this plant.
- **Dandelions** are a great green for a salad or can be eaten on the fly; they are full of vitamin A and the flower tops are edible as well. Dandelion root is a good coffee substitute when dried and ground.
- Young leaves of the **burdock plant** are especially good for salad greens, and the large taproot is fine starch.
- **Hickory nuts** can provide protein to your diet if you break them open and dig the nut meat from the inside.

- **Black walnuts** are a great source of protein and are not difficult to process. The hulls are useful for making a brown dye, and they have a chemical compound that when ground can be used to stun fish in small pools.
- **Raspberries** are very common summer fruits of the eastern woodlands. Other forms, such as salmon berries and black-berries, are common in other regions. These are a great source of fruit and vitamins and can be used in many meal applications and teas as well as eaten raw. Grapes are also common, although they have many poisonous look-alikes. The young shoots of these plants are also edible when fruit is not bearing, and the leaves make a good tea.
- **Common elderberry** fruits are very common from summer to fall. You can eat them raw as well as boil them to make a nice drink, or combine them with other foods to make a wonderful meal.

MEDICINAL PLANTS

Medicinal plants are also common, and many of them grow on roadsides and in yards all over the United States. Again, you should identify a few common ones that will help when used as simple remedies for common ailments, e.g., cold, upset stomach, headache, bites and stings, and allergic reactions (contact dermatitis). Plants that aid in hygiene are also worth understanding.

The following is a list of some more common medicinal plants:

PLANT	MEDICINAL BENEFIT
Cattail	antiseptic, tooth and gum care
Mullein	cold/congestion, female cycle needs
Jewelweed	contact dermatitis
Plantain	bites/stings
Mint	headache

PLANT	MEDICINAL BENEFIT
Mint and Dandelion	upset stomach
Yarrow	blood coagulant/cold and flu/insect repellent
Boneset	deep bruises, breaks, fevers

- **Charcoal:** This isn't, of course, a plant, but I mention it in this section as it can be an indispensable resource in the case of accidental food or plant poisoning. Ground in water, it will immediately induce vomiting and has absorbent qualities to remove leftover toxins from the stomach.

- **Cattail** has a very good gel that is present at the base of the sheath when the shoots are pulled out. This gel is anesthetic and antiseptic; you can liken it to aloe, as it is great for local pain relief from burns or stings. The young shoots of this plant make great toothbrushes as well.

- **Mullein** has been used for centuries as a decongestant and is great for cough and cold remedies; the large soft leaves of this plant can be used as wound dressings and are absorbent for female needs.

- **Jewelweed** plant has chemicals within its juices that help alleviate the symptoms of contact dermatitis from poison ivy and other plants. The freshly picked plant can be rubbed on the skin. It is important to use this plant as soon as possible after contact from a problem plant.

- **Plantain** can be used as a poultice by chewing the plant and then placing the macerated leaves on a sting or bite. It helps to draw out foreign objects such as splinters and thorns as well as the poison from a sting.

- **Mint** has many excellent properties for general and medical use. Fresh mint leaves rubbed on the temples will help ease minor headaches. Dried mint and dandelion infusions are good for an upset stomach and will help relieve diarrhea. A decoction of mint can also be gargled for sore throats, and an infusion or tea can be made with mint and yarrow to relieve cold and flu symptoms.

- **Yarrow** has been known throughout history for its abilities to clot blood from deep wounds; it also has anti-inflammatory properties. It will induce sweating when consumed as a tea and helps to break fevers. Recent studies have also shown that it's a great insect repellent.
- **Boneset** as an infusion will help break a fever, while a poultice of the green leaves will help with deep bruises and even bone repair.

USING MEDICINAL PLANTS

Medicinal plants are mostly used in four ways:

1. **Poultice:** By gathering the plant leaves and flowers raw and macerating them, you can form a poultice. This can then be steeped in boiled water or even chewed in the mouth (spit poultice) if it's an emergency, and then placed directly on the affected area and wrapped with a bandanna or bandaging.
2. **Infusion tea:** To make a tea or an infusion, steep as you would a poultice for approximately 10–15 minutes, and then consume the liquid after straining.
3. **Decoction:** A decoction is much like an infusion but requires the material to be boiled, not steeped. This method is used for any bark material or roots. The liquid is then strained and consumed after boiling half the liquid away.
4. **Wash:** A wash is an infusion used to clean the affected area, instead of ingestion.

PLANT/TREE AFFILIATION BY TASTE

If you know a plant is not poisonous, you can understand much about the properties by actually tasting it. Put it in your mouth, chew it up, roll it around; feel what it is doing on the palate and how it tastes. Based on taste, you'll be able to divide it into one of four categories:

- **Bitters:** Plants that have a bitter or acrid taste are generally good medicine for colds and flu. They will generally be both antiseptic and antiviral in nature.
- **Mucilaginous:** Plants that make the mouth water or are slimy will be good for constipation, as they will "grease the pipes," so to speak. They will be good for dry irritated sinuses, as well as burns.
- **Astringents:** Plants that are astringent will pucker your mouth or dry out your palate and will do the same thing in the body or on the skin. They will dry poison ivy, help dry up diarrhea, and cure a runny nose.
- **Carminatives:** These plants will feel warming or spicy, and will be great for stomach upset and general relief of gas and discomfort in the digestive tract.

Appendix C

BUSH
RECIPES

HARDTACK

4–5 cups all-purpose flour

2 cups water

3 teaspoons salt

1. Preheat the oven to 375°F (or 350°F if you have a convection oven or reflector oven).
2. Mix the flour, water, and salt together in a large bowl, and make sure the mixture is fairly dry. Add more flour if necessary.
3. Roll the mixture out to about ½" thickness, and shape it into a rectangle. Cut it into 3" × 3" squares, and poke holes in both sides with a fork or knife.
4. Place on an ungreased pan and cook for 30 minutes per side.

BASIC BANNOCK

1 cup flour (white or a mixture of white and whole-wheat)
1 teaspoon baking powder
¼ teaspoon salt
¼ cup dry milk powder
1 tablespoon shortening
Oil, for frying
Water, as needed

1. Make the mix at home ahead of time. Sift the dry ingredients together into a large bowl, and cut the shortening in until you have a granular, cornmeal-like mixture. Package this mix in zip-lock freezer bags. Double-bag it if you're going to be on a long trip.
2. Start with a small cast-iron or stainless steel frying pan and oil it well. You can also use a hardwood plank.
3. Pour approximately ¼ cup water into the bag and squeeze to mix.
4. Squeeze the mix out of the bag and into the warmed pan or onto a plank.
5. Your bannock will start to look loaf-like in 10–12 minutes, depending on the heat level from the burner. At this point you'll want to flip your loaf. To check for the finished product, take a toothpick and poke the loaf. If it comes out dry, it is done; if it comes out moist or with goo on it, let it cook some more.

SQUIRREL OR RABBIT ROAST

1 adult squirrel or rabbit
All-purpose flour, enough to dust the meat
Oil, for frying
Water, for roasting
1–2 potatoes, peeled and quartered
3–4 carrots, peeled and chopped
1 onion, peeled and quartered
Salt and pepper, to taste

1. Clean the meat well, making sure that all hair is removed. Cut into pieces.
2. Roll the pieces in flour and brown in the skillet (use just enough oil to keep the meat from sticking). Just brown the pieces; it is not necessary to cook the meat through.
3. When browned, add water to cover. Place quartered potatoes, chopped carrots, quartered onion, and salt and pepper to taste in the pot with the meat. Place the lid on the pot and cook over medium-low heat until done, approximately 30 minutes, depending on the heat of the fire.

FROG LEGS

12 frog legs
2 cups saltine cracker crumbs or ground hardtack
1 cup all-purpose flour
1 cup cornmeal
⅛–¼ cup diced onion
Salt and pepper, to taste
1 large egg
½ cup evaporated milk
Cooking oil or tallow, for frying

1. Rinse the frog legs and pat dry; set aside. In a large resealable bag, combine saltine cracker crumbs or ground hardtack, flour, cornmeal, onion, salt, and pepper. Shake to mix. In a shallow bowl, whisk together egg and evaporated milk.
2. Heat cooking oil or tallow in skillet over medium-high heat. The oil should be about ½" deep.
3. Dip the frog legs into the milk and egg mixture, then dip into the cracker mixture until evenly coated. Carefully place them in the hot oil. Cook until golden brown on each side, about 5 minutes per side. If the legs start to brown too quickly, reduce the heat to medium. Drain before serving.

BOILED BEAVER

1 hind quarter of beaver

1 large onion

3 carrots, sliced

2 teaspoons salt

1. Boil beaver in water in a large soup pot for 30 minutes. Drain and rinse. Repeat this method two more times.
2. Cover with water again, then add the remaining ingredients. Cover and boil until tender. Dispose of vegetables before serving, as they will hold most of the wild taste from the beaver.

MUSKRAT SOUP

Hind quarter of a muskrat
1–2 cups evaporated milk
3 boiled large eggs
1 tablespoon dried garlic mustard
1 tablespoon all-purpose flour
Black pepper, cayenne pepper, and salt, to taste

1. Cover the prepared muskrat (musk removed and thoroughly washed) with water in a large soup pot. Cook slowly until tender, adding water if needed, approximately 30 minutes, depending on the heat of the fire and the size of the quarters.
2. Cool, and take meat from bones. Cut meat into small pieces with a knife.
3. Save the pot liquor and add an equal quantity of evaporated milk. Mash egg yolks; add garlic mustard and flour, and stir into the liquid. Season to taste with black and cayenne pepper and salt, and return to a boil.
4. Chop the egg whites. Add the meat and egg whites to soup after it has boiled. Serve very hot.

RACCOON STEW

1 (4-pound) raccoon, cut into cubes
2 or 3 wild-picked onions, sliced
Salt and pepper, to taste
6–12 ground leaves garlic mustard, or to taste
Dash of hot sauce
Cubed potatoes and vegetables of your choice, to taste

1. Brown the meat cubes slowly in a Dutch oven, approximately 20 minutes. There should be enough fat within the tissues that no additional oil is required.
2. Add onions during the last of the browning process so they won't become scorched. Reduce the heat, season with salt, pepper, garlic mustard, and hot sauce, and cover. Simmer over low heat until almost completely tender, about 45 minutes.
3. Add cubed vegetables of your choice and continue to simmer until vegetables are tender. Serve hot with Basic Bannock.

BAKED DOVE BREASTS

12–24 dove breasts (approximately 1 pound)
Salt and pepper, to taste
2 cups all-purpose flour
Lard or tallow, for frying
¼ pound fresh mushrooms (morels), sliced
6 medium wild onions, sliced
1 cube chicken bouillon dissolved into 1 cup boiling water
Prepared brown rice, to taste

1. Preheat the oven to 350°F. Salt and pepper the dove breasts, and lightly flour. Brown in a cast-iron skillet with lard or tallow.
2. Place sliced mushrooms and onions on top of breasts. Top with the bouillon broth. Cover the skillet with aluminum foil. Bake for 25 minutes. Uncover and continue baking for 15 minutes longer.
3. Serve with brown rice.

SNAPPING TURTLE IN A POT

Salt, to taste
1–2 pounds turtle meat
2 teaspoons diced onions
⅛ teaspoon dried onion garlic
2 cups water
8 small unpeeled red-skinned potatoes, halved

1. Salt turtle meat well and place in your slow-cooking cast-iron pot. Add all other ingredients in the order given. Cover and cook on low heat for 6–7 hours or until turtle meat is tender.
2. Remove turtle meat from pot and cut into bite-size pieces. Return meat to slow-cooking pot, cover, and continue to cook on low heat for an additional 2 hours or until vegetables are done.

JERKY (ALL RED MEAT AND FISH)

3 pounds meat, lean cuts
Spices of your choice (salt, pepper, etc.)

1. Thinly slice the meat (as thin as possible; it will dry faster). Coat with ample seasoning by placing in a freezer bag and shaking.
2. Build a drying rack on your tripod and hang meat over a hardwood smoldering fire so that you can comfortably hold your hand in place over the rack for 3–5 seconds. Cover with a space blanket to make this process go faster and to create a smoking chamber as well.
3. Slowly feed the fire, avoiding large flames, until meat is dry enough to crack when it is bent. Store in a breathable bag for the trail. Rehydrate in soups for added meat value.

— Appendix D —
GLOSSARY

A-frame shelter
A shelter with two walls meeting at the top, which can deflect wind or rain from two sides.

aim off
In navigation, to take a bearing to the left or right of the intended destination by a few degrees so that you know, upon arrival at the bearing, to turn either right or left to get where you're going.

azimuth
A bearing, or the direction in which you are traveling; the angle of deviation of a bearing from a standard direction, such as north or south.

backstop
In navigation, a point beyond which you shouldn't go. Generally, a linear feature that runs perpendicular to your route to your intended destination.

bail stick
A form of pot hanger with multiple adjustment points so you can raise or lower the pot above the fire.

bank line
Tarred nylon used for fishing and net-making. It is a good survival cord as it is rot- and UV-resistant as well.

baseline
The opposite of backstops, baselines run perpendicular to your point of departure and provide a means of getting back to where you started from.

baseplate compass

A compass made from a flat plate that is usually transparent and can be laid on a map to determine accurate bearings.

batoning

A means of splitting wood by using a stick (or "baton") to strike your knife and drive it through a piece of wood such as a log.

bearing

In navigation, direction.

bezel ring

A movable ring on a compass indicating directions marked in degrees. It is used in orienting.

binding

Made of cordage, bindings are used to keep objects from coming apart or separating. For example, a binding on the end of a rope keeps the strands from fraying.

bird's nest

Used in fire-starting, this is a bundle of tinder shaped roughly like a bird's nest. It should be a combination of fine, medium, and coarse highly combustible materials.

bivvy bag

A plastic bag that covers the camper's head and sleeping bag to provide protection against wet weather or damp ground. Derived from the word "bivouac."

blood circle, the
In knife handling, the area 360° around you, farther than arm's length, where someone could come into contact with a blade being pushed away from the material being cut.

bow drill
A fire-making method that uses a bow to move a stick rapidly, generating friction and heat that can ignite tinder.

browse bag
A lightweight bag sewn up one side and across one end. It can be filled with material to make a mattress.

burner
The unit in a camp stove that produces the flame.

cable snare
In trapping, a snare trap made from steel cable.

canvas
Material used mainly for tarps and tarp tents. It is waterproof, usually fireproof, and mildew resistant.

charring tin
A tin box containing charred material to help in fire-making.

Conibear
A very effective trap for small animals and fish.

cranes
Made with a notched stick and a forked stick, cranes can be used to suspend pots over the fire or to hold anything else you want to suspend above ground level.

Dakota fire pits
A type of fire lay in which two holes are connected and a fire is built in one of them. The air circulating from the other hole keeps the fire burning hot and bright.

deadfall
Wood that has naturally fallen—dead branches, trees blown over, and so on.

deadfall traps
A trap that depends on the animal setting off a trigger that releases an object that falls on the animal, killing or trapping it.

debris hut
A shelter in which three corners are anchored to the ground, with one side mounted on a ridgepole, creating a triangular structure, which is then covered with leaves and other debris.

declination diagram
A diagram on a map that shows the amount of degree offset left or right between magnetic north and map north.

decoction
A drink made from material such as roots or bark, which is boiled, then drunk.

diamond board/diamond rod
A device for sharpening knives and other edged tools.

diamond shelter (plow point shelter)
Similar to a debris hut, this shelter is anchored by three corners to the ground, while the fourth corner is fastened to a tree or some other structure, thereby creating a diamond shape.

draw

The reduction in elevation from a saddle with high ground on both sides.

fatwood, pitch wood, lighter pine

The resinous area of the pine tree in which sap collects naturally. Excellent as fire-starting material.

feather sticks

Sticks that are cut to create bunches of shavings on one end. The additional surface area this creates makes feather sticks useful for starting fires.

fell

To cut wood, especially trees. Felling a tree is not a decision that should be taken lightly.

ferrocerium rod

A rod made from pyrophoric materials and used to start fires by striking it against a hard surface, which produces sparks.

fire lay

Wood laid in a particular pattern for the purpose of starting a fire.

flash tinders

Plant materials that contain volatile oils, which will readily combust. However, because of the fine fibers involved, they will burn very quickly and the flame is short lasting.

flying the tarp

A method of setting up a tarp in which none of it touches the ground.

ground cloth/ground pad
A cloth or blanket you can lay on the ground to protect yourself against damp and cold.

hammock
A bed you can swing between two supports off the ground. It keeps off creatures and prevents the loss of body heat through conduction.

handrails
Linear objects within the terrain that you can use as a guideline to follow when they lead in the intended direction of travel.

haversack
A small bag you carry on one side of your body. Used for items that are likely to be of immediate importance.

hemp
The tough fiber of the Indian hemp plant, used for making cordage.

jackknife
A pocketknife in which the blade and other implements fold into the handle.

juglone
A poison that prevents or stunts the growth of many plants. It can also be used in a concentration for a fish-stunning potion.

keyhole fire
A fire pit dug in the shape of a keyhole. The fire is built in the "hole" and hot coals are dragged into the trench to form a cooking area.

kindling
Material that can be easily ignited to start a fire.

knife grind
The shape of the cross section of a knife blade. Different grinds require you to hold your whetstone at different angles when sharpening the blade.

kuksa
A cup (also known as a noggin) made of wood or plastic. It can be used for drinking or cookery.

lashing
Knots used to fasten several objects together. They're essential in constructing sturdy shelters in the wild.

lateral drift
The tendency, when walking long distances, to gradually move left or right.

lean-to shelter
A shelter made from a single wall propped up at an angle and covered with leaves, branches, and other debris to form a secure roof.

log cabin fire
A fire lay made by laying logs crosswise in a square with kindling and tinder inside.

L.U.R.D.
Left, up, right, down. A method of navigating based on the apparent movement of the stars due to the earth's rotation.

magnifying glass

A lens used for close examination of anything as well as a reliable firestarter in the wilderness.

map scale

An indicator of the correspondence between measurement on a map and real distance. For example, some maps may indicate that one map inch equals one mile of distance.

military Modular Sleep System (MSS)

A set of sleeping bags—one intermediate weight and one light-weight—and a bivvy cover, that provide sleep protection in most environments.

mule tape

A tape much used by electricians, which has a very high tensile strength and is lightweight.

notching

Carving notches in a branch or pole, either for construction or to create hangers and handles.

oilcloth

A waterproof cloth used for tarps and tents, made of cotton coated with mineral spirits and linseed oil.

pace beads

Strands of beads used to keep track of distance while walking. You drop a bead on the strand after walking a given number of paces.

pan tension

The amount of tension required to move the pan of a trap down and spring the trap.

parachute cord
A cord that has a woven outer covering (the mantle) that protects the inner strands that give the cord its strength.

PAUL method
Standing for Positive Azimuth Uniform Layout, this method will allow you to scout an unknown area and figure a straight line bearing back to camp without backtracking by reverse azimuths all the way.

pitch a camp; strike a camp
Set up a camp; take down a camp.

pitching the tarp
To stake any part of a tarp at ground level.

planks
Slabs of wood crosscut from a larger piece and used as a cooking surface for foods such as breads and bannocks.

polypropylene
A lightweight material that can be purchased very inexpensively; however, its longevity and durability make it unsuitable for anything other than the short term.

poultice
A soft, moist mass that's applied to the body as a bandage or a remedy for illness.

resection
Taking a bearing using triangulation to determine your location.

resin

The sap of a pine tree. It has various uses, including as a firestarter, bandage for a wound, and various medicinal purposes.

ridgeline

A series of hilltops, offering an observation point and high-ground travel.

Roycroft frame

A frame for carrying your pack. It consists of three sticks lashed together to form a triangle.

rucksack

Another name for a backpack. This is the basic bag in which you carry most of the items you'll need while in the wilderness.

saddle

A lower-lying area between two hilltops that forms a drainage point for the hilltops as well as protection from wind and rain.

shear cut

A cut made with the intention of shearing off wood from a larger piece.

sheath

A case or covering for a bladed tool.

silnylon

Nylon impregnated with silicon, making it waterproof.

sleeping bag
Any of a number of padded bags made for sleeping. They can be insulated with feathers, down, artificial insulation, or air space, among other things.

strop
A device, often a leather strap, for putting a fine edge on a blade.

tannin
An astringent derived from the oak tree. It can be used to make poultices, infusions, and dyes.

tarp
Short for tarpaulin; a canvas or oilskin covering, used to erect shelters and for other purposes in the wild.

teepee fire
A fire lay in which kindling is stood on end with the tips touching, looking like a teepee.

tinder, tinder bundles
Highly combustible material that can readily take a spark or easily catch fire when a smoldering ember is added.

toggle
A wood stick or dowel connected to a line by a knot. This can be used as an attachment point that is easily moved or removed, and will be load bearing if needed.

tomahawk
An axe with a slender, straight handle that can be easily removed, making it a hand tool that can be used for other tasks.

Trangia stoves
A stove in which an enclosed material wick (usually asbestos) is sealed in a confined space with holes at the bottom of the container for alcohol to wick in.

triangle of death, the
The part of your body that should always be shielded from a knife or axe. It comprises the space between your upper legs, including the groin and both femoral arteries.

tubular webbing
Webbing used primarily for climbing. It weighs less than rope, takes up less space, and generally has higher tensile strength.

tumplines
Straps for a pack or frame that are worn across the forehead to assist in carrying heavier loads.

upland trapping
Setting traps above the water on higher ground for animals such as coyote, fox, raccoon, opossum, and other small land animals.

Venturi effect
The tendency of air entering a narrowing tube to flow faster. This can have a significant effect on a fire.

whetstone
A stone used for sharpening or honing a bladed tool.

widowmakers
Standing dead trees that may easily fall or break if subjected to wind. These could cause serious safety issues.

ABOUT THE AUTHOR

Dave Canterbury is the co-owner and supervising instructor at the Pathfinder School in southeastern Ohio (named by *USA Today* as one of the top twelve survival schools in the United States). He is an army veteran and currently a self-employed hunting guide and survival instructor. His work has also been published in *Self Reliance Illustrated*, *New Pioneer*, and *American Frontiersman*.

INDEX